FIFTEEN MINUTES AGO

FIFTEEN MINUTES AGO

A VIETNAM WAR MEMOIR

CRAIG TSCHETTER

MCP - Maitland

Mill City Press, Inc.
2301 Lucien Way #415
Maitland, FL 32751
407.339.4217
www.millcitypress.net

Printed in the United States of America

ISBN-13: 978-1-63505-636-5

To my wife, Della.
To my children, Jennifer and Mark.
To my granddaughter, Tatum.

Author's Note

This is a memoir. The accounts you will read are true. While the events occurred over forty years ago, significant diligence was employed to ensure truthfulness. My resources included a personal diary, multiple discussions with marines I served with, letters my parents saved, tape recordings I sent home, and unclassified information from two Vietnam archive centers. The names of military operations, locations, and units are, to the best of my knowledge, accurate. Conversations are written as I remember them and not necessarily verbatim. The book contains terms and language that may be unacceptable in many settings but they accurately represent my experience of the war, so I feel it's important to include them. Some names have been changed to protect the privacy of individuals.

PREFACE

In March 2013, my son, Mark, and I took a trip to Vietnam. I had a desire, before I died, to return so I could once again smell the air, walk the ground I had so hated, and observe the people under communist control. The small travel group of twenty consisted of mostly women my age, and a few of them brought their spouses. I was one of two veterans and the only one who served in Vietnam, a point of interest for others that spurred a great deal of questions. Even our guide, named Thuyen (pronounced Twin), was prone to asking my opinion about events during what he referred to as the "War with America." It appeared that everyone, except me, took whatever Thuyen said regarding the war as gospel. Of course, I would whisper his inaccuracies to Mark. I was surprised at how naïve people were about a time that was so pivotal in my life.

An example of one inaccuracy occurred on the day the bus traveled north on Highway 1 from Saigon (Ho Chi Minh City) to Hoi An. As the bus passed the road leading to the village of Trang Bang, he began to tell the story of the famous photo of the *Napalm Girl*. He said, "Her name is Kim Phuc, and the famous photo was taken on June 8, 1972, by Nick Ut, a Vietnamese war photographer. In the photo she's the nine-year-old child running naked on a dirt road and crying as her home and village burn in the background." The picture appeared on the cover of *Life* magazine and eventually earned Nick Ut a Pulitzer Prize.

What Thuyen did not tell the group was that the bombing of civilians was committed not by the United States but by the South Vietnamese Air Force. I could hear members of the group commenting about how terrible the act was and questioned why would "we" do such a thing? Thuyen continued with the history of Kim Phuc and encouraged everyone to read her book titled, *The Girl in the Picture*.

When we arrived at Hoi An and departed the bus, I waited beside Thuyen so together we could walk to the hotel. I politely asked, "Thuyen, why did you not tell the group the plane that dropped the napalm was flown by a South Vietnamese pilot and, instead, lead them to believe it was an American pilot?"

He stopped, looked at me, and said, "I know that, but your country supplied the napalm."

"Thuyen, do you really believe we would supply napalm to kill innocent civilians?"

"I don't know; it was your napalm." He walked away.

Later that evening before the group left for dinner, Mark and I joined him on the patio for a drink. He was sitting alone reading on his laptop. I asked him about a place I had feared during my time in Vietnam called Ga Noi Island. He hadn't heard of it but decided he'd look it up. When he turned on the laptop, my name appeared on the screen, and he quickly picked it up. Obviously, he had Googled me to see what my background was and to determine if I was ever in Vietnam during the war. He found no reference to a place called Ga Noi Island, but he now knew I had been a United States Marine. From that time on, Thuyen and I got along very well.

A few days later the bus entered a large plaza filled with tourist buses and with people busy shopping for souvenirs. Some were beautifully crafted while others were merely a waste of money, but while we were there Thuyen found a person he wanted me to meet, one of the other bus drivers. Thuyen knew he had served in combat with the NVA (North Vietnamese Army) during my time in Vietnam. (Thanks to his laptop he had read my tour dates.) When the former NVA soldier and I met, the not-so-happy guy looked at me, and I looked at him. He was dressed in U.S. Army fatigues with the former owner's name ripped off above the right shirt pocket and a North Vietnamese cap with a Red Star. We continued to stare at each other like two dogs ready to pounce. He finally said something to Thuyen in Vietnamese. I asked Thuyen, "What did he say?"

Thuyen hesitated, but the man insisted he tell me. Thuyen replied, "He said, he kill marine, and marine shoot at me."

I told Thuyen, "You tell him he's one lucky son of a bitch."

Thuyen hesitated again, but told him, which produced a penetrating expression.

He also wanted me to know he fought in the area around Phu Bia during the Tet of 68. I thought, *That's where I was too.* Following a short photo shoot by members of our group, we reluctantly shook hands and went our separate ways.

Mark said, "How'd that feel, Dad?"

I replied, "Not very good."

Thuyen told me later the driver wanted me to know he wore both the U.S. uniform and the NVA hat to show we are now same-same.

I thought, *You've got to be kidding me.*

NVA soldiers with author in Vietnam 2013

* * *

James F. Dunnigan and Albert A. Nofi published a book in April 2000 titled, *Dirty Secrets of the Vietnam War,* filled with myths, statistics, terminology, and every sort of information on the war one could want to know. The pair also published other books regarding WWII detailing similar information both from the Pacific and European Campaigns.

Of all statistics found in the book, the one at the top of page eighteen is by far the most profound: "During the Vietnam War period, about 8.7 million Americans served in the Armed Forces. Only some 2.6–2.8 million of them were sent to Vietnam and fewer than 300,000 served in the bush under fire. So if you went into the armed forces during the Vietnam era, your chances of being shot at regularly in Vietnam were about one in thirty."

As I look back on the trip, I feel a sense of having fulfilled a part of my life I would have always regretted had I not taken it.

At no time did I see the journey as a means of gathering information for this book, but as it turned out, the journey provided me with some of the Vietnamese people's silent thoughts on views of the *War with America*—insight that at times produced frustration, anger, and some good feelings about our two countries. Yet, it's hard to forget the days of bitter fighting and the tremendous loss of human lives inflicted on both countries. It may have truly been for nothing—for nothing.

I shared with Mark my perception that it would be very easy for people on the bus to think the *War with America* was Vietnam's only conflict; most of our traveling companions seemed naïve. The fact is, the Vietnamese have been fighting foreign rule for thousands of years. The Chinese first held Vietnam for 1,050 years, until 936 A.D. The Champa ruled for a few years and eventually yielded it back to the Chinese. In 1257 the Mongol empire invaded and held on until being defeated in 1287. The next few hundred years were filled with fighting among the Vietnamese in the name of religion and land. Then in 1856 the French entered the picture with the hope of saving the Catholics from persecution. Eventually, they colonized the country, claiming their rule. During WWII, the Japanese pushed the French out and occupied the ports to support their war effort. The French reclaimed the country after WWII (with financial aid from the United States) and were finally defeated in 1954.

The United States involvement began in the fifties, and in March of 1965, U.S. Marines landed on the beach near Da Nang. In every single case, the Vietnamese people paid with human lives. The people on our trip had no idea how long and hard this country has fought to be independent. Some would say the millions of lives they lost is the true tragedy of Vietnam and its people. I would have to agree.

Author with son Mark at hotel in Saigon, Vietnam

ACKNOWLEDGMENTS

I have been blessed in this endeavor by many people I consider friends and scholars. There are also those special people, my family and closest advisors, who stood with me and supported me during this process. It is to these people I owe a special acknowledgment.

To my beautiful and enormously patient wife, Della, for her support; to my daughter, Jennifer, for her hours of help with legal advice, reviewing, and transcribing documents; to my son, Mark, and his partners/staff at Feynman Group for developing my website; to Sharon King Wieczorek for her endless hours of editing; to Chuck Cecil for his encouragement and assistance with photo editing; and to Mary Alice Haug for her advice on publishing. For all these people I have a great deal of appreciation. It's because of their support that this book came to fruition.

—Craig A. Tschetter, Author

Introduction

"Warriors deal with death…they take life away from others…this is normally the role of God… asking young 19–20 year-old warriors to take on that role without adequate psychological and spiritual preparation can lead to damaging consequences." —Karl Marlantes, *What It Is Like to Go to War*

The morning sun warms the back of my neck as I sit with my head resting on my forearms. I stare at the hundreds of brass shell casings and grenade pins scattered about the foxhole. Along with my squad leader, Corporal Larry Mahan, and another marine, I have occupied this position since 8:30 last night. I've been sitting here alone trying to sort out the events of the past two days in order to have them make sense, but I can't. Maybe things don't make sense during war. It's just all messed up. I wish I knew.

Slowly I lift my head and glare at Mahan's evil eyes as he takes a hard drag on his cigarette. He sneers: "Be careful checking those bodies; they may be booby trapped."

I'm his radio operator, which means I'm stuck with him. But I hate him. I hate him because of what he did yesterday, and I hate him for the position he put me in. I wish the bastard was dead.

Today is January 31, 1968. India Company is south of Da Nang in a small hamlet called Lo Giang 2. I'm exhausted, hungry, and have no words to describe my feelings about what is on the ground in front of me. I open my plastic canteen and pour some water on my bloody, snot-infested neck towel to wipe my face. After pouring the rest on my head, I stand up to survey the carnage.

Scattered across the ground in all directions lay the dead bodies of Vietnamese soldiers along with what they carried when they overran our company's positions last night. Pieces of arms, legs, and viscera dangle from trees; other pieces lay strewn atop shrubs. I had no idea we killed so many. A quick count reveals fourteen lay in front and three to the left of our position. Could it be possible the three of us killed all seventeen?

Gradually, I shift my eyes to the one body I'm certain I killed. He's still lying in the same position I remember from last night, so he must be dead. I have no idea how many more are dead because of me. But who gives a shit anyway? The truth is I'm alive and they're not.

The same scene exists throughout the village, along the river bank, and in the open field adjacent to the hamlet.

For the marines of India Company, this no-name operation will, in the months to come, be known as *The Alamo*. Yes, we played the role of God last night when we took life away from one hundred and two Vietnamese soldiers, and yes, we will do it many more times. We will do it because our country's leaders asked us to, and we innocently agreed. Right or wrong—we agreed.

In 1967 I volunteered to join the military in search of a way to leave home. I didn't understand the meaning of discipline, courage, or patriotism—let alone how four years of military duty would change my life. I was trained to be a warrior. I did "God's work" in the mountainous jungles and rice paddies of Vietnam for twenty months. I participated in patrols, ambushes, five-man killer teams, and search-and-destroy missions. I killed enemy soldiers because it was my job and watched while friends died senseless deaths, leaving me to wonder when it would be my turn. Eventually, I became a walking, half-awake, jungle-rot-infested zombie just like everyone else. I have no idea the number of booby traps I walked by or the number of sniper and machine-gun rounds I averted. There's no way I can count the hot landing zone insertions or extractions I survived and the number of mortar and B40-rocket rounds I eluded.

Friendly fire from misguided air strikes and incorrect artillery coordinates killed far too many marines around me. So it's no surprise I kept asking myself, *Why not me? When is my life going to end?*

They say, "War is hell," and I suppose it is. However, combat, which not every soldier experiences, goes far beyond hell. Far too many people believe war implies all military personnel carry weapons and engage the enemy. This is simply not true. Many military personnel in combat zones are never issued a weapon, let alone fire one. Veterans of war are not necessarily veterans of combat, a gravely misunderstood fact of war.

In the fall of 1980, the effects of combat began to take control of my life. I fell into a deep dark hole of depression that appeared to have no way out. Often, I found myself sitting alone in tears, chasing the images and thoughts of combat that wouldn't leave my mind. At the peak of my depression, I made the decision to end my life. Out of fear of what I might do to myself, I sought help from the Veterans Administration hospital in Sturgis, South Dakota. With the help of the Veterans Administration doctors, I began a journey of recovery through counseling, through medications, and through writing. I found the hope and desire I so desperately needed to begin living a meaningful life.

During the past two decades, I have considered putting these words on paper numerous times, and each time I have failed. I have struggled with why anyone would care about my stories or my efforts to deal with PTSD (post-traumatic stress disorder). I toiled for hours about how to portray my feelings, thoughts, and flashbacks about Vietnam so readers could understand them. It was hard and, honestly, I may have failed, but it gives me great pleasure to know I've finally completed the task.

I wrote this book seeking to heal my soul from my ghosts of war. I also wanted to give those I love a greater understanding of war and the residual effects it can cause. Plus, I trust it reveals the naïveté youth often experience about the grandeur of becoming a combat soldier, unaware of the damaging consequences it will cause. Unfortunately, it's never a topic of discussion by recruiters, even though it should be.

The short stories or incidents in this book are some of what I think about every day. They are some of the daily forces persuading me to crave solitude. They are my ghosts of war. They are what have caused my severe panic attacks, sudden bursts of anger, anxiety, and thoughts of suicide. They are the residual effects that a combat soldier must eventually learn to accept. Why? Because they keep warriors up at night filled with remorse, guilt, and fear.

CHAPTER ONE

"Everyone has to make their own decisions. I still believe in that. You just have to be able to accept the consequences without complaining."
—*Grace Jones*

W hen I was born in 1948, my parents represented the blue-collar workers who were so common after World War II. My father, fresh out of the Navy, worked fourteen-hour days for a small dairy, bottling milk, making butter, and packaging cottage cheese. It was hard work, but in those days a job was far more important than a paycheck, so he took whatever he could get. His only qualification for the job was that he grew up on a South Dakota farm, but to my mother's brother who hired him, it made little difference. The two veterans got along well and, at times, according to my mother, too well.

Mom and Dad bought their first home in the early fifties. It was small, with a dirt basement and no grass in the yard. Mom cleaned that house every week to perfection. She was so proud of our home. My father spent no time with household tasks; his jobs were the yard and washing the car. In 1955 a semi loaded with sod was parked on the gravel road next to our house. Dad along with some of his friends worked for three days making our bare yard green. It was beautiful, and I was proud. We finally had green grass.

Following her father's death, Mother left school after the eighth grade to help at home. She was seventeen when she married Dad; they spent just three days together before he shipped out to the South Pacific Island of New Caledonia for twenty-two months.

"I can still remember standing at the train station in Huron waiting for this stranger to return," she would say. Having been married now for forty-some years myself and knowing what I know today about being apart, the reunion must have been difficult.

Mom grew up on a flatland farm surrounded by a large, loving family. Her father was a highly regarded community member and devout Christian. He regularly expressed his strict Mennonite beliefs to his family and taught them the word of God as gospel. Today, my mother is ninety years old and firmly believes every word of the Bible to be true.

My father (who died in 2012), on the other hand, was raised Lutheran, and by all accounts, lived a life much less confined by doctrine. He graduated from a small high school in Wolsey, South Dakota, and really never thought much about religion. I've always thought it a bit odd that my parents actually found each other and married. Maybe my mother's sister dating my father's brother was reason enough for them to marry. My parents' union provided for a strange mix of beliefs. Mother's idea of worldly vices collided with my father's Navy ways. Dad smoked and enjoyed going to the pub; Mother worked and prayed.

On September 23, 1953—one of the happiest days in my mother's life—my father made an abrupt turn and became a born-again Christian. The drinking and smoking stopped, the nightlife disappeared, and he became obsessed with the word of God. Life changed for everyone in our house, dramatically.

Dad became a deacon at Mount Olivet Mennonite Church. Within a few years, he was on the Board of Directors of James Valley Christian High School. He rapidly ascended to an icon in the Mennonite community; he savored every minute.

For both children and adults, Sundays began with Sunday school, usually lasting one hour. Worship service added another two hours before we returned home to a house filled with the smells of Sunday dinner. The scriptures called for Sunday as a day of rest, therefore the afternoon activities were very restricted. Playing outside was okay, but certainly did not include anything such as hunting or spending the day at a friend's house.

By 7 p.m., we were back in church for the evening service for another two hours. Thursday evenings were spent attending youth services followed by choir practice. The routine was seldom broken. The older I became, the more I hated it. I hated it for more than just those reasons; I hated it because of the unforeseen events that plagued my life.

On one occasion my sister, Marlis, claimed she couldn't sleep because she was so concerned for me that she went to my parents' bedroom in tears. My father hailed me out of bed to come downstairs to the kitchen. When I entered the room, there sat my parents and my sister.

"What's happened?" I asked.

Then, I noticed the open Bible in front of my father, and I knew I was being accused of some awful thing and my sister must have turned me in. I'd been through this drill more than once, but what did I do?

My father spoke first, "Marlis said you are hiding a deck of playing cards upstairs. Is that true?"

I looked at her, and she burst into tears. I quietly said, "Yes."

Having playing cards in the Mennonite faith was a major sin because they represented the Devil (somehow) and possession of them was a big enough deal to require a biblical discussion. Yet, I was tired and just wanted to go to bed. It was nonsensical.

After the incident, my sister and I didn't speak for quite some time. In situations like those, she would always apologize by saying, "I didn't know what I should do, so I did what I thought was best for you."

After my sophomore year in the Huron public school system, my father decided I should attend James Valley Christian High School, located thirteen miles north of town. As a member of the Board of Directors, he believed his children needed to be educated in a Christian environment. He claimed the foundation for all future endeavors such as college, marriage, and a career required a biblical background. I struggled to make sense of what my parents believed, and, disappointingly, they couldn't see how their beliefs were affecting me.

I was no longer seeing life as normal, but instead as a burden of unwanted religious mandates. I began to harbor negative thoughts about my parents and religion. I felt a desperate need to get away. I truly loved my parents, but I wasn't going to allow their religious convictions to control my life.

Following graduation in May of 1967, I entered the Huron Post Office seeking information on the military. The branch of service wasn't important. I just wanted to get away from home, and the military seemed like the best answer.

The Army recruiter's door was locked, and the Air Force recruiter had a sign posted: "Out to lunch." Standing alone, I saw through an open door at the end of the hallway a man sitting in a white uniform. I recognized the uniform from my dad's WWII pictures, and I decided to join the Navy. Standing rigidly in front of his desk, I introduced myself and asked, "What's the quickest way to get to Vietnam?"

Stunned, he placed a phone call and handed me the receiver, "Here, you're talking to the United States Marine Corps in Sioux Falls, South Dakota."

I thanked the man in white and left. Walking home, I began to rehearse how to tell my parents my intentions. I quickly decided my decision was final, regardless of what they might say. After all, I didn't need their blessing; I was eighteen.

Following evening dinner, I broke the news, catching them completely off guard. They glared at me in disbelief and struggled for words. Mother asked, "Why? What about Vietnam? You could be killed."

Looking at Dad I said, "I want to serve my country just like you did." He left the table without saying a word. I knew I had broken my mother's heart; yet, my father's actions fueled my decision even more.

On June 13, 1967, I enlisted in the United States Marine Corps for six years—four years active and two years inactive.

The following week my family drove me to Omaha, Nebraska, where I boarded the Santa Fe train for my journey to the Marine Corps Recruit Depot in San Diego, California. I was excited just thinking about becoming a United States Marine and serving my country during a time of war. No one could have changed my mind. Years later, I realized the carelessness of my decision.

I have often thought about my uncle Ken, sitting on my bed, asking me, "Why the Marine Corps? The Navy or the Air Force would give you hot meals, a bed, and a roof over your head."

I responded, "Because I want to be a marine and serve my country."

Today, I understand what he was telling me. Maybe I should have listened.

CHAPTER TWO

Boot Camp doesn't turn young men into killers. It removes the societal restraints on the savage part of us that has made us the top animal in the food chain." — *Karl Marlantes, Author*

I was alone, free, and excited. It was my first time on a train. I felt confident. More appropriately, in 1967, I felt cocky— and I loved it. Three days later my swagger changed to anxiety when the train rolled into San Diego.

A tall, mean, tough-looking marine wearing a Smokey the Bear hat awaited a fresh batch of recruits. Standing as stiff as the creases in his uniform, hands affixed to his hips, hat tipped forward, impressive rows of ribbons on his chest—he gave off a daunting command for respect. He was unmistakably the most fearsome person I had ever seen. As we young civilians stepped off the train, he shouted for those joining the Marine Corps to form a line in front of him. Standing straighter than ever before with my butt cheeks compressed, I felt proud about becoming a marine like he was. He walked up and down the line slowly stopping to stare with disgust at each one of us.

G/Sgt. B. Kealoha

Author's Boot Camp Platoon Commander 1967

"Listen Up! No one forced you to be here. No one held a gun to your head when you signed enlistment papers.

Civilian life is over: you now belong to the United State Marine Corps. So guess what, girls? I own your fucking ass." Fear of the unknown began to overtake my body.

Upon arrival at the MCRD (Marine Corps Recruit Depot), I was herded with everyone else into the receiving barracks where I was stripped of my civilian identity. Wedding bands and wallets could be kept.

Except for confiscated contraband like knives, brass knuckles, and magazines, everything else was to be shipped home. I folded my clothes just like Mom had taught me, placed them neatly in the box, and closed it.

After a quick shower, we dressed in the issued white boxers, white T-shirt, green utility trousers, cap, socks, and black boots. We stood in rows, with our noses placed on the back of the head in front of us, until sometime after midnight. Gunnery Sergeant Kealoha finally returned and moved the formation into a large room on the second floor and gave orders to find a rack to sleep. The huge room smelling of cleaning solution went dark; the only light came from the San Diego moon. I felt scared and alone as I stared at the ceiling for hours questioning why I wanted to be a marine. I had no answer.

Three hours later the lights came on when three drill instructors burst into the room yelling:

"Get your asses up!"

"Get up, you fat sons of bitches."

"Get up, you miserable pieces of shit."

"Get your asses outside on the yellow footprints, *now*!"

"GO! GO! GO!"

So shocked, I wasn't even sure I was dressed when my boots covered the yellow prints painted on the asphalt denoting proper foot placement. The barking drill instructors used every foul word known to man. Fuck was the word of choice, and they used it in every possible vernacular. At times guys would laugh at a drill instructor's "jargon;" they quickly learned that was a dreadful mistake. Drill instructors had no mercy for recruits who questioned their routine or their language.

Within a short time, we were marched to the barber shop where, in thirty minutes, seventy recruits were sheared bald. I stood outside in formation with hairs itching my neck and shoulders.

A few guys dripped blood from moles that had been carelessly whizzed off their head. The guy standing in front of me soiled his trousers—the smell was stomach-churning. He was soon discovered, grabbed by the throat, slapped across the face several times, mocked, and positioned behind the platoon. He remained there, humiliated, in his soiled trousers for the rest of the day. The actions of the drill instructors put the fear of God in me. I couldn't tell if they truly hated recruits or if they just enjoyed being ruthless. One thing was for certain: I was going to do my best to avoid trouble during my eight long weeks of training.

The yelling and harassment from drill instructors during the first two weeks proved relentless. Some recruits were beaten for no valid reason, causing me to become even more uneasy. I found myself trapped in an environment where I was genuinely concerned for my life. So psychologically stunned and overcome with fear, my bowels didn't move for seven days.

Panic overcame me one night when I heard my name called to report to the duty hut. The duty hut is where drill instructors lived, and no one ever looked in the door for fear of mysteriously being struck dead or maimed for life. I recall thinking someone must have died or possibly there was an emergency back home. I quickly dressed and ran to the door of the duty hut. Slamming the metal plate with the metal flapper three times, I jumped to attention and yelled at the top of my lungs, "Sir, Private Tschetter reporting as ordered, Sir."

No response.

Again, I went through the same sequence and this time heard, "Get in here, you piece of shit!"

Finding myself in the forbidden zone of the duty hut fearing for my life, I snapped to attention in front of the drill instructor's desk and locked my eyes on the wall. SSgt. Reeves said, "What the fuck is this shit?"

My eyes went from the wall, to the desk, and back to the wall. "Sir, Cookies, sir," I said.

"Well, no shit, you four-eyed fuck."

He then gave me two minutes to eat every cookie. It was not humanly possible. I knew it, he knew it, but ultimately I began shoving cookies down. When the time expired, my mouth was still jammed with cookies. He slowly approached me, slid in front of me, and placed his nose against my nose. His foul Camel cigarette-smelling breath consumed my face as he screamed, "What a putrid, worthless, piece of shit!" He guaranteed I would "never be part of his Marine Corps." Then, out of nowhere came a crushing blow to my gut, producing a huge explosion of puke. Somehow he had ducked clear of the flying yuk and slammed me to the floor. I covered my head with my arms and curled into the fetal position as he violently began kicking my body.

"You miserable piece of shit."

"You son of a bitch."

"You miserable piece of shit; you fucked up my house!"

He ordered every inch of the hut cleaned—even if it took all night. I cleaned for hours before my bruised body painfully collapsed on my bed. Alone and confused now, I once again lay staring at the ceiling wondering if I would ever be a marine. And, wondering why, why, my cousin Claudia, who had never sent me anything in my entire life, would send me cookies.

Boot camp is designed as a training ground to instill discipline, motivation, and teamwork in order to be part of an elite fighting force. It exemplifies the old saying: the more you sweat now, the less you bleed in combat. To validate the importance of teamwork, I quickly realized one recruit's blunder resulted in the entire platoon paying a price. There was no greater trigger for this torture during our boot camp than Private Kenneth L. Worley. The amount of physical punishment he placed on Platoon 396 was beyond measure. Not a single recruit, including me, liked him or cared as we watched him being beaten week after week.

At times the drill instructors had him watch as the platoon suffered through endless sit-ups while we hurled sand into the air, causing sand to rain on our sweat-soaked bodies. Amazingly, for Pvt. Worley, the ridicule, beatings (called "thumping"), and the hatred seemed to have meant nothing. He took it all and never said a word.

Tschetter, Craig A.
Turner, Willie A. Jr.
Vattuone, John J.
Waldroup, Michael F.

Worley, Kenneth L.
Yeager, Randall L.
Skulrat, Vichien
Jacobson, L. E.

Pvt. Kenneth L. Worley and Author's Boot Camp photos 1967

* * *

Later, Kenneth L. Worley from Farmington, New Mexico, served with Lima Company, Third Battalion, Seventh Marines, as a machine gunner in Vietnam. On August 12, 1968, while on a squad-size ambush, he threw himself on an incoming enemy grenade to save the lives of his fellow marines. He was posthumously awarded the Medal of Honor for his unselfish act.

The first time I read his citation I was astounded. Not a single recruit or drill instructor would have guessed Private Worley, our biggest shit bird, would one day receive our nation's highest honor. It seemed impossible.

One might ask how is it possible to take young men off the streets of America and in eight short weeks make them capable of giving their lives for a fellow marine. In the forward of William Mares's book titled, *The Marine Machine*, General David M. Shoup, the twenty-second Commandant of the Marine Corps and a WWII Medal of Honor recipient, described it best: "Young Americans are tedded into this Marine curing process by the drill instructor. His role is to be grossly misunderstood, much maligned, hated, cursed, until one night in faraway jungle foxholes, anticipating the landing of the next enemy mortar shell, many of these same recruits, grown to manhood during their first days of combat, mumble in reverence, 'Thank God, Sergeant Jones was our DI at boot camp.' Strange though it may be, this reverence will remain with them until death, whether in combat or in the relative calm of later civilian years."

I humbly believe the indestructible bond developed by recruits during boot camp is the powerful force that forever links marines. Worley might not have shown his emotions during boot camp, but he clearly understood the meaning of being a United States Marine. He clearly exemplified the Marine Corps motto, *Semper Fidelis, Always Faithful.*

* * *

The eight weeks of harassment, thumping, and physical suffering finally ended, and I was officially given the title, United States Marine. Graduation day proved remarkable to me because I had accomplished what weeks earlier my drill instructor told me would never happen. I observed families and girlfriends proudly gathered around their young marines celebrating the special day. For me the day was full of pride and achievement; however, I was without anyone to share it with.

My only phone call home during boot camp was two weeks before graduation. Members of the platoon were given the opportunity to invite family and friends to graduation. My parents told me it would not be possible for reasons they couldn't or wouldn't explain. With a lump in my throat and covering my eyes filled with tears, I left the phone booth.

Several years later I returned to MCRD with a close friend and his family to attend the graduation of their son, David. I had strongly encouraged them to make the trip because I knew what it would mean to David, as well as his family. They were all extremely proud of David and rightly so. I wanted David to experience what, for some reason, my parents couldn't give me.

The Recruit's Creed states: "To Be A Marine You Have To Believe In Yourself, Your Fellow Marine, Your Corps, Your Country And Your God." The day I graduated, I believed in myself more than ever before, but it would take the jungles of Vietnam to teach me how to believe in my fellow Marine, my Corps, my Country, and God.

Medal of Honor. Worley, Kenneth L.

Worley, Kenneth L.

Rank and organization: Lance Corporal, U.S. Marine Corps, 3d Battalion, 7th Marines, 1st Marine Division (Rein), FMF.

Plate and date: Bo Ban, Quang Nam Province, Republic of Vietnam, 12 August 1968.

Entered service at: Fresno, Calif.

Born: 27 April 1948, Farmington, New Mexico.

Citation: "For conspicuous gallantry and intrepidity at the risk of his life above and beyond the call of duty while serving as a machine gunner with Company L, 3d Battalion, 7th Marines in action against enemy forces. After establishing a night ambush position in a house in the Bo Ban, Hamlet of Quang Nam Province, security was set up and the remainder of the patrol members retired until their respective watch. During the early morning hours the marines were abruptly awakened by the platoon leader's warning that 'grenades' had landed in the house. Fully realizing the inevitable result of his actions, L/Cpl. Worley, in a valiant act of heroism, instantly threw himself upon the grenade nearest him and his comrades, absorbing with his body, the full and tremendous force of the explosion. Through his extraordinary initiative and inspiring valor in the face of almost certain death, he saved his comrades from serious injury and possible loss of life, although five of his fellow marines incurred minor wounds as the other grenades exploded. L/Cpl. Worley's gallant actions upheld the highest traditions of the Marine Corps and the U.S. Naval Service. He gallantly gave his life for his country."

CHAPTER THREE

"As long as there are people who will kill for gain or power or who are simply insane, we will need people called *warriors* who are willing to kill to stop them." —*Unknown*

Infantry Training Regiment (ITR), where the battalion endured four weeks of intense combat training at Camp Pendleton, followed boot camp. Located thirty miles north of San Diego, Camp Pendleton was lush with deciduous trees, rugged hills, and arduous training facilities. It was the largest Marine Corps installation. In 1967, ITR was shortened from eight weeks to four in order to provide more troops for Vietnam—the same reason boot camp was shortened from twelve weeks to eight. Training was limited, but concentrated.

During ITR, I was taught the nomenclature and firing procedures for every weapon that would be available to me in Vietnam: hand grenades, claymore mines, M60 machine guns, M50 machine guns, M79 grenade launchers, M72 light anti-armor weapons, and assorted rifles and pistols. Firing of weapons was done over and over again until actions became routine. During this training, I began to feel like a real warrior. I could taste what it must be like to actually use these weapons against the enemy.

Additionally during ITR, I was promoted to Private First Class (Pfc.), instilling in me an awesome sense of pride. Later that day, I found it came at a severe price. In 1967 the Marine Corps still practiced a form of hazing called "pinning stripes," essentially a severe form of physical torture for making rank.

Two columns of marines spanned the length of the barracks just wide enough apart for a marine to walk between them. One at a time, the promoted were forced to walk the gauntlet as each marine of equal rank or higher "pinned his stripe."

As hard as possible, the marines' fists pounded the arms and legs of the promoted, forcing them to stagger or fall from the onslaught of thuds. Some didn't make it halfway before falling to the floor in tears. Others would try to escape only to be beaten far worse than if they had walked the line. I stumbled through the line but could barely lift my arms or walk the next morning. Pfc. Beck whose rack was next to mine couldn't stop crying because of the beating he had suffered. (Eventually "pinning stripes" was outlawed by the Marine Corps.)

Following ITR, I was sent home for two weeks of much needed leave. I was anxious to see my family and friends and to share my experiences as a marine. Because my parents worked, I spent most of my time with high school buddies discussing boot camp, ITR, and Vietnam.

My parents seemed uninterested in what I had to say, and when they did ask a question, I sensed that they just wanted me to feel like they cared. My two brothers, on the other hand, wanted to know about everything.

They were especially interested in the postcards I sent them from ITR depicting night firing of machine guns with red tracer rounds. As kids we would play combat outside at night, simulating machine-gun fire, throwing grenades, and killing our make-believe enemy. Now, they had a brother who had actually fired real weapons and was going to war. I could see the pride in my brothers' eyes, making me even more willing to serve.

Two weeks passed quickly and the time came for me to leave. Realizing this might be the last time I'd see my family, I felt sad—for both them and me. Interestingly, I felt no fear, and did not shed any tears. I was willing to go to war and, if need be, die for my country.

Returning to Camp Pendleton for what the Marine Corps called "staging battalion," I entered the final phase of training before deployment to WestPac (Western Pacific, or Vietnam). During those three weeks, we experienced realistic combat scenarios: going on day and night patrols, setting up various ambushes, and searching mock villages. We received specialized training on booby traps, enemy weapons, and Vietnamese phrases.

They made certain we understood the Geneva Conventions regulations, Rules of Engagement, and what to do if we were captured. Most of all, they made certain we understood how to kill the enemy. They taught us various methods, using techniques or technology, to terminate a life. We practiced day after day to make killing become routine.

I began to realize the importance of boot camp, infantry training, and now staging battalion. Everything made sense. I was going to Vietnam to further our country's containment policy; I would fight to ensure that communism would stay within its existing borders and not spread to Vietnam. I also clearly understood I was going to a hostile environment where killing or not killing the enemy meant I would either live or die. Yet at no time did any of the training make mention of the potential psychological side effects relevant to combat. The emphasis was always kill or be killed. Ultimately, we were trained to be part of a highly synchronized unit designed to inflict lethal force.

I was absolutely convinced my training would provide me with the safety net I needed to survive in Vietnam, but I didn't yet know that in Vietnam there was no safety net. Survival was up to me; I needed to learn how to survive and learn as fast as possible.

CHAPTER FOUR

"Don't wait to introduce yourself to the Lord, get
to know him now. In combat you want to be on
a first-name basis." —*Joe Rippetoe*

Two days after battalion staging ended, my name
appeared on a flight manifest scheduled for WestPac.
I left El Toro Air Force Base in California for Camp Butler in
Okinawa, with a stopover in Hawaii for fuel. I can still see
the Pan American stewardesses in blue and white uniforms
strutting with sexuality throughout the twenty-two-hour flight.
I felt their sincerity and willingness to do everything possible
to make us feel proud of our commitment and to ease our
concerns about the tragedies of war.

When the plane landed in Da Nang, one young stewardess addressed us over the PA system. Her voice wavered
as she wished us all the very best—and a safe return. Then,
with enthusiasm, she said, "Everyone is entitled to a departing
kiss." The plane erupted in cheers and applause. Not a single
marine passed up the offer and some, like me, kissed all five.

Leaving the plane, I felt edgy about this strange, foul-
smelling, and mysterious country. The line outside the
receiving hangar seemed to go on forever. I wondered where
I would be sent and to which unit I would be assigned. An
hour passed and then another until I finally made it inside
the air-conditioned hangar filled with marines, most were
chattering about being assigned up north near the DMZ
(Demilitarized Zone). The air conditioning provided a much

needed reprieve from the tormenting humidity and heat outside. Still, I was uncomfortable.

The hangar, made of corrugated steel, had several large fans humming overhead, and it appeared to be some type of briefing room for pilots. On a raised platform at one end, staff shuffled through papers, conversed hastily, and appeared overwhelmed. Speaking through a bullhorn, a staff sergeant began to call names of marines who were to be picked up by personnel from the various battalions. Within the hour, my name was called along with six others to be assigned to the Third Battalion, Fifth Regiment of the First Marine Division.

A loud voice suddenly shouted, "Three-five over here." Keeping a close eye on the arm waving for three-five, I immediately walked away from the guys I was talking to and worked my way through the crowd. I didn't recognize any of the others gathered for the Fifth Marines.

Outside the hangar a truck called a "six-by" was waiting to take us to the base camp. The truck resembled a dump truck with wooden benches below the side rails. Behind the cab stood a weary-looking soldier manning a fifty-caliber machine gun mounted on the cab's roof. Draped over his flak jacket was a belt of ammunition that partially covered the large inked words: *Get Some.*

Another marine reached down for our sea bags and flung them into the truck. Once on board, he handed out helmets, flak jackets, M16 rifles, and two magazines of ammunition. Looking at everyone to make sure we had all our gear, he said, "Gentlemen, lock and load. We have fifteen miles to go and it's *not* secure."

Black diesel exhaust filled the air with a foul smell, and the truck slowly began to move. While getting organized, I noticed my weapon was covered with some sort of crud. I smelled it, scraped it with my fingernail, and concluded it was dried blood. A quick glance at the other weapons told me mine wasn't the only one.

I couldn't stop looking at the dried blood and wondering about it. *This was someone else's weapon. He may have been killed or wounded. Why would I be issued a used weapon?* It made no sense to me. Months later it would become profoundly clear.

A few miles outside of Da Nang, the truck came to a stop behind two trucks parked alongside the road. The driver, unarmed, jumped out of the truck and disappeared behind small Vietnamese hooch's. To me they looked like family dwellings, so I had no idea what was going on. Finally, the machine gunner said, "Don't worry, guys, we'll be moving soon; it's just bad-ass gook pussy!" I glanced at the others, shrugged my shoulders, smiled, and continued scanning the countryside for trouble.

By late afternoon, a small area filled with bamboo trees, several plywood buildings, and sandbag bunkers strategically placed around the perimeter—the remote base camp (named An Loc)—finally came into view. I could see a small landing pad made of pierced steel, two tall wooden watchtowers, and dirt roads where marines calmly walked about. I didn't know that the camp, my home for the next two months, was by far the safest camp I would occupy.

An Loc base camp 15 miles south of Da Nang 1967

Sgt. Earl Schultz arrived to claim what he called "three fresh bodies flowing with warm blood for India Company." For some reason, staring at this rough-looking soldier gave me a sense of security.

"Where's everyone from?" he said.

He gave me a warm smile when I said, "South Dakota."

As we walked to the India Company area, he asked about my hometown, about my family, and if I played sports. He, too, was from South Dakota, and I was the first marine he had met from home. Suddenly, I felt comfort; I realized I wasn't alone anymore.

He told the group we would receive an extra forty-five dollars a month for what was called hazardous duty pay. Everyone chuckled.

"Wait till you get your ass shot at; you'll see it's not fucking near enough."

No one said a word.

Once we arrived, Sgt. Schultz assigned each of us to a squad leader within second platoon. After the other two left he said, "I'm assigning you to my best squad leader, Corporal Hanley." I believe he did this because I was from South Dakota. Regardless, he made me feel special, and I thanked him for his kindheartedness.

Cpl. Hanley made me feel as comfortable as possible for a newbie flowing with warm blood. The men in second squad, on the other hand, seemed cold. When Hanley mentioned I was from South Dakota, things changed. My guess was they either liked Sgt. Schultz or they were afraid to mess with someone from his home state. I never did find out, but I was grateful.

A marine combat company, such as India, was comprised of three, forty-five-man platoons. At full strength, a platoon consisted of three squads of twelve led by a squad leader, for a total of thirteen. The remainder of the platoon was composed of weapons platoon personnel, such as machine gunners and mortar men. The platoon commander, usually a second lieutenant, with his personal radio operator, completed the full platoon component. The three platoons, plus weapons platoon and headquarters/supply personnel comprised a complete company; roughly two hundred men.

Each squad had its own quarters, consisting of a large tent set on a raised wooden platform. The screened sides were covered by flaps that could be rolled up to allow for airflow, or lowered during the monsoons. Both ends had a wooden screen door that banged shut by a heavy spring, and that led to three wooden steps. Squad members occupied small areas along the screened sides. Each area consisted of a cot, poncho liner (lightweight silk blanket), and several empty ammo cases stacked for shelving. Gear and personal items were stored under the cot, leaving the wide center aisle free of clutter. Officers shared their own tent, which was furnished much the same.

Following squad introductions, Hanley and I sat down on my cot, and he briefed me on several items: "Your required gear is being brought over from supply. Make sure you inspect it thoroughly." Being prepared, he explained, was important because I would be going on patrol the next day. He also told me to clean my weapon because it "looked like shit."

A squad patrol returns through the south gate at An Loc in 1967 Three hole crapper with open doors to remove burn barrels of waste

He went on, "When the base gets hit by rockets or mortars get the hell out of the tent and find a bunker."

Then he looked me square in the eyes and said, "I want you to understand something, marine. It's not a matter of *if* you'll get hit or *when* you'll get hit, it's just a matter of how *bad*."

I stared at him without saying a word. He stood up and walked out the banging screen door, leaving me with the disconcerting "welcome to Vietnam" message.

My eyes began to tear up; my head dropped into my hands. I felt afraid. I'm certain no one saw my tears, but I was overcome by what he said. Later that night I realized he wanted me to understand that life is uncertain in this environment. More importantly, he needed me to accept that sooner rather than later.

To pass my time before morning, I checked and rechecked my gear and thoroughly cleaned my M16. Sleep was impossible. The strange sounds, strange smells, and strange people left me feeling insecure. Thoughts of how to survive for thirteen months and of being surrounded by total strangers overwhelmed me—total strangers I desperately needed to prove my worthiness to and not embarrass myself as a coward. Yet, I had no idea how.

The next several weeks continued to be unsettling as I struggled to adjust to my surroundings and to my fellow marines. It seemed that every week brought a new event and subsequent series of thoughts that seemed impossible for me to comprehend.

On my fourth day in country, a huge explosion rocked the base inside of the perimeter. Marines yelled, "Incoming." I flew out of the tent into a bunker and hunkered down waiting for the next round to land. No other round came and by morning it was clear why. Mike Company's first sergeant had been murdered by a disgruntled marine who detonated several pounds of C4 under his quarters. He had killed him because he had given his R&R (Rest and Relaxation) trip to another person. *How could one marine murder another?* It made no sense.

A week later, I found myself standing in company formation while a Vietnamese family scoured the ranks looking for their daughter's rapist. I have no words to describe how I felt when they stared at me. I actually can't recall if the person was ever found, but I know for certain, he wasn't part of India Company.

That same week Pfc. Deblak blew off his lower arm while examining a souvenir he had brought back from the bush. The hidden explosive inside the Chinese communist grenade (Chi-com) had been in our tent for weeks. I think every guy, including me, handled it at least once. When it exploded, several of us who were standing and talking outside the tent ran to help him. Just before he passed out he said, "My hand is gone! My hand is gone!" Someone else said, "Shit! He got his ticket home with just one hand."

Two weeks later, I was exposed to friendly fire for the first time. An 81-mm mortar round fell short and landed inside the perimeter. The direct hit on a tent occupied by members of weapons platoon resulted in three killed and thirty-five wounded. After that night, every HI (Harassment and Interdiction) round fired tormented me.

Days soon turned to weeks as day patrols mixed with night ambushes consumed my life. It was frustratingly difficult to maintain alertness because of fatigue. Everyone was always exhausted, bitchy and on edge. The good news was the squad liked me, making me feel part of the team. However, I had yet to prove myself, and I knew it.

CHAPTER FIVE

"Combat is fast, unfairly cruel and dirty. It is
meant to be that way so that the terrible experience is branded into the memory of those who
are fortunate enough to survive so they can
pass it along to those who just might want to
try it." —*Unknown*

On December 28, the company received orders for a major
operation code-named "Auburn." India Company's
mission called for insertion by chopper into Landing Zone
Hawk with orders to form a blocking position to assist Echo
Company, Second Battalion, Third Marines. Echo's orders
were to sweep a village named Bao An Dong located near LZ
Hawk. The village was one of many located on Ga Noi Island,
a place I would learn to fear in the months to come. It was
home to the NVA's Second Division along with VC Battalions
tagged R-20 and V-25. They were well entrenched within
bunkers both above and below ground—and they loved to
kill marines.

Hanley called the squad together for a quick briefing,
which amounted to: "We're going to the island, so get ready
for some shit. Ammo and C-rations will be at the LZ; take
what you need."

The chopper ride from our base camp to LZ Hawk went
quickly. I recall feeling pumped and cautiously ready for
action. When the CH46 helicopter tail ramp dropped open,
Pfc. Cox was the first squad member to jump. He dropped
immediately. Enemy machine guns were zeroed in on every

chopper's tailgate. Suddenly, my gung-ho emotion changed; I hesitated to jump. I was looking down at Cox when someone yelled, "Move! Move!" Quickly, I jumped over him into the knee-deep rice-paddy water and stumbled for cover near a large embankment.

As the remaining squad members jumped, not realizing Cox was there, they continued to step on him. I thought for sure he was dead. To everyone's surprise, he had tripped and planted his face in two feet of rice-paddy mud. Finally, he got up and sloshed his muddy body to the squad's position while machine gun rounds zipped the water around him. He was more mad than hurt. We still laughed about it weeks later.

Cpl. Hanley moved the squad to our preplanned position where we set up firing positions. The scene produced a drama of orchestrated confusion. Choppers circled overhead with more troops to off-load. F4 Phantom jets were dropping two hundred and fifty-pound bombs on a tree-lined hamlet five hundred meters away. The bombs shook the earth with such force I could feel the impact followed by a blast wave—hauntingly exhilarating to me.

Soon the company was ordered to move closer to a heavy fire fight outside the village. Our move required us to pass through six-foot-tall elephant grass, which, unknown to India Company, was filled with enemy snipers. Before long they had us pinned down, and we were straining to see the marine next to us.

Once we moved through the grass, Cpl. Hanley informed us that Lt. Corr had been killed by a sniper. The loss of our platoon commander was hard on everyone. I later learned, Sgt. Schultz carried him in his arms to the LZ and gently laid him in the row of other dead marines. Schultz was his platoon sergeant from the day he took command in July. To most of us, Sgt. Schultz was never the same after Lt. Corr's death. He had lost a respected, personal friend.

I remember thinking an officer being killed seemed strange. What I didn't understand then was that officers—and their radio operators—were preferred targets for snipers.

Operation Auburn was the first of nine battalion operations I participated in from November 23, 1967, to July 27, 1969. Auburn was unique in that it was the only operation in which I served as a rifleman. It was also my indoctrination to combat, firefights, and facing death first hand.

Experiencing combat was unlike anything I'd ever felt before. Everything was happening so fast and with such confusion that I found my role hard to understand. I became concerned about measuring up to Cpl. Hanley, as well as the rest of the squad. On the second day, Cpl. Hanley placed me alone by a large mound and told me to establish a field of fire to my right. He said, "I'll be back in a while to check on you."

I didn't even question him. I did exactly as he said even though I was alone, an easy target, and had yet to fire my weapon at the enemy.

A couple hours later he returned and pulled me back to within the squad, making me feel more secure. The feeling didn't last long as soon all hell broke loose. It was as if he knew it was going to happen. Mortar explosions threw deadly shrapnel everywhere and enemy machine gun rounds zinged the ground, leaving puffs of dirt where they hit. Without regard for incoming explosions and machine-gun fire, platoons opened up with devastating gun fire. Their mortars continued landing; our machine guns, M79 grenade launchers, and M16s kept firing, making it impossible to hear the marine next to you. It was a collection of weapons blasting, men yelling, loading and reloading of guns—and fear.

I fired magazine after magazine into the tree line even though I never once saw a confirmed target. Then, it was over. Everything became quiet.

Hanley yelled, "Everyone okay?"

Responses confirmed the squad was fine. Even though I was still shaking, I had never felt such a rush of adrenaline. I had been indoctrinated in combat. I had been put on the cusp of death and survived. I felt like part of the squad; I did my part by finally firing my weapon, even though I didn't kill anyone. I felt confused and thought I needed to play a bigger role but had no idea what that meant.

Later that night I helped carry a dead marine to the newly established landing zone. I'm not certain the body was from our battalion, but several bodies in one area needed to be moved for tactical reasons.

The dead were always considered the least important medevac but still needed to be taken out before dark.

Six of us grabbed the rubber poncho holding the dead marine and began our slow walk to the LZ. He was heavy and awkward to carry for six out-of-step marines loaded down with gear. I couldn't stop looking at the large hole in his head and his mangled body. There was no doubt he had been killed by shrapnel. I kept thinking, *Why him and not me?*

Near the halfway point, someone in the back lost his grip and we dropped him. When we picked him up again, his lower leg fell off into the rice-paddy water and sunk. The piece was quickly pulled from the water, examined, and pitched on his stomach with an alarming thud. Once we reached the LZ, we laid him in line with the other dead and covered him with the poncho. I'm certain I will never know his name, but his image is still with me today.

On December 31, the "organized confusion" came to an end. Cpl. Hanley pulled the squad together to explain extraction orders. Amazingly, after four days of at times intense combat, second squad was unscathed. I wondered if Sgt. Schultz had been right about Cpl. Hanley being his best squad leader.

Operation Auburn ended at a price of twenty-three marines killed and sixty-two wounded. Of the twenty-three killed, Echo Company lost seventeen. India Company lost three: Lt. Corr, Pfc. Murphy, and Pfc. Townsend.

When we returned to our base camp, I spent the rest of the day cleaning gear and trying to make sense of what I had just lived through, replaying those four days over and over in my head still trying to understand my role. Just before dark

Cpl. Hanley, at Sgt. Schultz's request, came to check on me. He told me that Sgt. Schultz would be the new platoon commander until another officer could arrive.

He also wanted me to know I handled myself well and wondered if I had any questions. I said, "No."

After he left, I wished I had asked him why I felt so uninformed about second squad's role in the operation. It didn't take me long to realize only a few people received briefings—the rest just participated, never really understanding the mission.

Later in the week, I requested to walk point on the squad's next patrol. I knew the point man was always briefed about the patrol, so why not take point? Hanley looked at me curiously, slowly nodded his head "yes," and walked away without saying a word. I found his actions odd but assumed he had other things to worry about.

I didn't sleep well that night but felt confident I was ready to lead the squad on patrol. Not only did I walk point the next day, but I also walked point the next two days—once at night. Walking point is the loneliest and most terrifying duty any foot soldier can experience. I felt like I was wearing a flashing sign that read, "*Shoot me first*" so those behind me would have a fighting chance. There are no words to describe the courage it takes to lead those who are depending on you for life's protection. Someone has to be first, but I quickly realized it didn't have to be me.

Following three patrols walking point, I told Cpl. Hanley I would like to carry the radio. I didn't care it weighed twenty-three-and-a-half pounds; I just knew the radioman always followed a squad leader, a platoon commander, or a company commander—none of whom ever walked point. After two weeks of carrying the radio for Cpl. Hanley, he officially declared me second squad's RTO (radio telephone operator).

Within a week of returning from Operation Auburn, Second Lieutenant Tom Saal took command of the platoon. Like Lt. Corr, he was a small man, cropped his hair close, and possessed unquestionable confidence. I felt a deep respect for officers, and this one proved no different. Lt. Saal would soon promote me, educate me under fire, and build my confidence to a new level. I only hoped that one day I could repay him for the knowledge and confidence he gave me.

CHAPTER SIX

"In war more than elsewhere things do not turn out as we expect. Nearby they do not appear as they did from a distance." —*Carl von Clausewitz*

January began with the close of Operation Auburn and ended with the beginning of the infamous Tet Offensive. My position as the squad's radio operator gave me an incredible sense of worth—something I badly needed. My confidence in my fellow marines was at an all-time high. I lived one day at a time; I understood yesterday was gone and tomorrow may never come. At only nineteen, I had become keenly aware of life's uncertainty.

Monday, January 15, was no different than any other day, hot and muggy. By 3 p.m., second platoon had been briefed, saddled up (gear on), and was ready to board choppers for what Regimental Command called Rough Riders Duty, a code name given for rapid-reaction forces and also referred to as Sparrow Hawk (small units) or Bald Eagle (company size) missions. Marines called them suicide runs because they were outrageously dangerous. Whoever designed the duty certainly never participated in one but obviously believed tactically the strategy should work.

Rough Riders Duty called for a certain-size unit to be positioned at a given landing zone (ten hours per day) with choppers armed and ready to insert troops once an enemy location had been confirmed by an AO (aerial observer).

Within minutes of a sighting, marines would board the choppers and depart to the target.

The object was to surprise the enemy, hit them hard, and when the mission was over, radio command for extraction. Everyone traveled light: no food, limited water, but all the ammo he could carry, usually an extra two hundred rounds.

The concept sounded simple, but I along with everyone else knew nothing ever happened as planned. This time would be no different.

Four CH46 choppers lifted off from the battalion base camp at 3:50 p.m. carrying second platoon under the command of India Company's commander, Captain Henry Kolakowski, Jr., who we all called Captain Ski. The ride was short to First Recon headquarters in Da Nang, which served as the platoon's home for the next six days. The recon marines lived much better than bush grunts, so I considered this a bonus. Once the ten-hour stint ended, I grabbed a hot meal, a shower, and relaxed the rest of the day. No night ambushes or day patrols to deal with. Life was great. It was great for the first three days, and then on day four, it all changed.

Around 2 p.m., an OV-10 pilot spotted an estimated seventy-five NVA soldiers in a small hamlet hiding what he assumed were weapons and rice. He immediately alerted the command center. Moments later the chopper rotors started to turn, and the word was passed to saddled up. My stomach began to churn, my heart pounded faster, and I could feel the rush of anxiety. I checked my grenades, radio, and ammunition and followed Hanley aboard. Once airborne, I found myself struggling with menacing thoughts about life and death.

Bald Eagle operation 1ˢᵗ Recon LZ January 1968 CH46 chopper

Our target grid was a short thirty minutes away, so everyone quietly rechecked his weapon. The crew chief signaled two minutes: time to lock and load. All eyes stayed with the crew chief waiting to see if the LZ was hot: no signal. Two Huey gunships prepped the hamlet with rockets just in case of an ambush. The four choppers landed side by side in an open dry rice paddy within fifty yards of the hamlet. Searching for what the OV-10 pilot reported, squads rapidly dispersed throughout the hamlet.

The only people I could see were local villagers. They appeared scared yet friendly. No one fired a shot, no NVA were captured, and for all practical purposes, it seemed like a false sighting, but...

"Weapons, we got a shit- pot full of weapons." Soon more and more weapons and rice were uncovered with the help of local villagers. The only question was who did the AO (aerial observer) see? Something wasn't right, and Captain Ski knew it.

AK47 rifles, B40 rocket launchers, and rice were piled in bunkers and destroyed with several pounds of C4 explosive.

In the Skipper's mind, the village was NVA, even though the civilians had tipped us off to some weapons. Yet, where were the NVA soldiers?

Over two hours passed before Captain Ski radioed Command for the extraction team. They informed him that cloud cover had grounded all choppers and extraction would have to wait a day. He was frustrated—no, furious. He knew the situation all too well and didn't like the odds. During the initial briefing he was told there could be two hundred NVA, but the observer couldn't tell for sure. Our strength was less than fifty. If everything had gone according to plan, the mission would have been perfect. Not this time.

When Captain Ski briefed the squad leaders, he made certain everyone understood the situation. He said, "*No one sleeps. Two-man foxholes: dig deep and make the perimeter tight enough for voice communication. NVA outnumber us four to one, and no one can get to us if we are overrun.*"

Not a single person slept, no one even fired a shot, and at daybreak as the fog began to burn off, I was sure our luck had changed. At 8 a.m. I informed Cpl. Hanley (having overheard the radio message) that Command assured the skipper that choppers could fly within the hour. The good news traveled quickly, and everyone felt relieved except for Captain Ski. He knew the NVA were in the area and probably used the night to plan their attack.

As word came that the choppers were airborne, the squad leaders were ordered to the CP (command post). Hanley and I quickly moved to the CP for extraction orders.

Ski said, "We'll keep as much fire power on the ground as possible, allowing for one squad to lift off at a time. The gunships and remaining birds will circle overhead providing supporting fire. The command post and second squad will be on the last bird. Corporal Hanley, keep two machine gunners on the ground along with two riflemen until the end."

Walking back to the squad, Hanley said, "Why are we always the last bird?"

I said, "No shit."

Before long, I could hear the sound of approaching choppers, which gave me a small sense of relief. They were quickly overhead and circling just as Captain Ski had said, gunships included.

Soon the first chopper landed, loaded, and lifted off. The perimeter quickly moved together to fill the gap. Then the second bird landed, loaded, and departed. Again the perimeter adjusted to close the hole created by the absent squad. The third bird landed, loaded, and lifted off without a shot fired.

Hanley whispered to me, "This is too easy, something is not right."

Finally, the last bird sat down, and the rest of us loaded. Then we waited for the last four to pull away from the perimeter.

Once the final four boarded, the pilot throttled up, and we began to lift. Suddenly, the chopper was pounded by small arms fire. The NVA soldiers piled out of the trees firing on full automatic. The number of NVA was unbelievable, and they kept coming like pissed-off bees leaving a hive. Gunships fired M60 machine guns and rockets, while the circling CH46 choppers fired their 50-caliber machine guns trying to hold the gooks in the trees but to no avail.

Inside the chopper, second squad was in mayhem. Hot casings from M60 machine guns, M16 rifles, and 50 calibers bounced in all directions. Scalding hot, they landed on arms, legs, and necks, burning tissue with ease. The sound of guns firing filled the air; guys were yelling for more ammo, while others sharing windows kept firing. AK47 rounds were zinging through the fuselage and pounding the engines with extreme accuracy.

Once we cleared the LZ, the shot-up chopper scraped the tree tops for ten minutes, crossed over the Cam Ha River, and then hit the ground.

Everyone knew we were going down. There was nothing to do but hold on to the canvas benches and hope the chopper didn't explode. It hit the ground with a thud; rotor blades shattered as they tore through the earth, throwing grass and dirt in all directions. Wheels buckled. Fix-mounted

50-caliber machine guns broke off their supports, ripping the fuselage and falling to the ground. As I began to scurry out, I noticed the marine next to me was covered in blood; he wasn't moving. Two of us dragged him to the gunner's door and fell to the ground. He grimaced with pain as we moved him to a secure area away from the chopper.

I was certain the chopper would explode, but it didn't. The crew chief quit counting hits after nineteen because there were too many up by the engines. The pilot claimed he started losing oil pressure just after he lifted from the LZ. He told Captain Ski it could have been a lot worse; one B40 rocket and none of us would have survived. Captain Ski's "After Action" report stated the NVA were no doubt there to resupply with weapons and rice, but the surprise attack left them to scatter empty-handed.

A medevac came for the one wounded marine. Before long I was on a truck headed to First Recon happier than hell to be alive.

Someone asked Captain Ski, "Who thinks up this shit?"

He removed his helmet, rubbed his sweaty head, and said, "Some dumb son of a bitch who never landed in or left a hot LZ."

We all laughed. For some reason it was funnier when he said it because, as the CO, he probably knew the dumb son of a bitch.

The platoon returned to our base camp on January 20, having never flown another mission. I was grateful to be back running night ambushes, day patrols, and living in shitty conditions.

Other India Company members would ask us what Rough Riders was like. The routine response was "Exciting—you should try it" or "It's fun." Two weeks later the entire company was assigned a Bald Eagle mission. It was a mission no one would ever forget.

Sometime in January, Cpl. Hanley received orders to rotate back to the states. His twelve months and twenty days had finally arrived, and he was going home. I hated to see him leave, but I was happy he survived.

Sgt. Schultz assigned Cpl. Larry Mahan to lead second squad, and his leadership style couldn't have been more different. He intimidated me, and his gung-ho attitude drove the squad into a deep-seated hatred for him. As his radio operator, I was forced to hang with him in the bush—even though I didn't trust him. My feelings were confirmed two weeks later: the day my life changed.

CHAPTER SEVEN

"Something in me died at Peleliu. Perhaps it was the childish innocence that accepted as faith the claim that Man is basically good. Possibly I lost faith that politicians in high places, who do not have to endure war's savagery, will ever stop blundering and sending others to endure it." —*Eugene B. Sledge, USMC*

Fourteen miles south of a village called Lo Giang 2, *I* lay on my cot drifting in and out of consciousness. A light breeze comforted my body. I had been in this sleep state since the squad stumbled into camp shortly before dawn. I was exhausted and in desperate need of rest after conducting day patrols and night ambushes for two consecutive days. Typically, squads only operated for fourteen-hour periods, but Cpl. Larry Mahan, our medal-hungry squad leader, volunteered us for the forty-eight-hour assignment, reinforcing second squad's hatred for him.

At 8:30 a.m., the screen door at the end of the tent crashed open and Mahan barked, "Listen Up, Listen Up! Get saddled up; squad meeting out front in thirty minutes. Take all the ammo you can carry, two canteens, and no chow. Supply's bringing over more ammo, so load up." He turned on his heel, and the screen door slammed shut behind him. Everyone, including me, sat on his cot, stunned, looking at the screen door and wondering what that son of a bitch had volunteered us for now. Cpl. Skaggs (fire team leader) yelled from across the tent, "Bird, is there any traffic on the net?"

The squad had started calling me Bird because I began rolling my jungle utilities up to below my knees, exposing my skinny legs. I often heard, "Hey Bird, what's the word?" Marines thought radio operators knew the latest to happen, and, in many cases I did, but I seldom shared.

"Nothing," I replied without checking.

I liked Skaggs, but he questioned everything and far too often volunteered an opinion, only making matters worse.

Private First Class Jackson, whose canvas cot was next to mine, quickly asked, "What do you think, Bird?"

"Shut up and get your shit ready," I snapped.

Pfc. Roy Jackson, by marine standards, was small in body, but made up for it with bravery. He humped a BAR (Browning automatic rifle) almost as long as he was tall and at twenty-six pounds, just as heavy as it looked. His diet consisted of chewing tobacco chased with Kool-Aid, and he hadn't stopped talking since arriving two weeks ago. Even though he never shut up, I liked him; actually, I liked him a lot.

Pfc. Cox was out the door first and started grabbing grenades and frantically loading M16 magazines. Directly behind him, Pfc. Whitmore did the same, followed by Lance Corporal Soliz. I positioned the radio in my pack, flipped it up onto my back, and left the tent to grab some ammo. Cpl. West and Pfc. Jackson were right behind me.

The squad was busy checking gear, loading magazines, and crimping pins on grenades when Mahan arrived with the briefing. "All right, listen up! This is a Bald Eagle mission involving the entire company. The best information I have is an AO spotted an estimated two hundred Viet Cong in a small village south of Da Nang. It's believed they're staging for a rocket attack on Da Nang's airstrip. The company will be inserted near the village and take up blocking positions to trap them. There's a river on three sides of the hamlet, so they either swim or die. Air and artillery are prepping the area now, so move out; the choppers are waiting."

Mahan yelled, "Bird, get over here." As we walked toward the choppers, he said, "Listen, whatever you do, make damn sure you stick on my ass; this LZ will be hot." I confirmed the order.

I saw squads from all three of the company's platoons walking to the LZ as staging began for boarding. "Is Lieutenant Saal here?" I asked.

"No, Sergeant Schultz is in command. Lieutenant's in Da Nang."

"Lucky him," I said. He ignored me.

When I finally sat down on the narrow canvas jump seat, I could feel the powerful engines as they rumbled my small, overloaded body. Beside me and always ready to be the first out was Mahan; I would be right behind him. Suddenly my stomach sank as the pilot throttled the engines and the bird lifted, tipping its nose down to gain altitude while racing forward. Within seconds we were airborne with the cool outside air blowing through the circular windows. My bulging pack prevented me from leaning back against the fuselage, so I sat with elbows on my knees holding my M16 vertically with both hands. Some of the squad's eyes were closed as if sleeping or praying. Mahan was plotting artillery grids on his map for quick reference. Jackson, as usual, was talking, but Soliz could have cared less. Cox appeared nervous. He kept taking his magazine in and out of his M16 to check the rounds. I wished he would stop before he accidently chambered one and shot a hole in the bird.

The wind felt good as it fluttered my clothing; my T-shirt was becoming soaked with sweat. The roar from the big engines was mesmerizing, causing me to lower my head as crazy thoughts churned in my mind.

Is today the day I die?

Someone always dies.

God, I wish I'd eaten breakfast.

Home, I wonder what's going on back home?

Before long the chopper began to slowly descend, moving the ground closer and causing hearts to beat harder and faster. Looking out the large tail ramp, I could see other choppers descending and realized we would soon be on the ground.

I kept thinking, *Stay with Mahan. Stay with Mahan.*

The hydraulics started to grind and the ramp began to lower. Instantly, the nose lifted and the big bird touched ground, bouncing forward, sideways, and finally settling. Within seconds the entire squad was out of the chopper and running for cover through a cloud of dust. I was on Mahan's ass just as he ordered. Thirty yards later, squatting down in a long ditch, he yelled, "Head count!" Everyone was present and accounted for.

Overhead, F4 Phantoms screamed down on the village, dropping two hundred and fifty-pound snake-eye bombs and napalm. The ground shook with every explosion. Smoke lifted as fires burned in the village; the odor penetrated my nostrils with an all-too-familiar smell of a hamlet on fire.

Strange—there was no incoming, at least not yet.

A few minutes passed before Sgt. Schultz radioed for the squad leaders to report to the CP. I relayed the message to Mahan and together we took off, leaving the squad in position. Schultz's briefing was quick and to the point. "Once the prep is done, we've been ordered to move out. We will secure the area from the wire fence to a large ditch in the center of the village. First platoon has two KIA (killed in action) and several WIA (wounded in action). The only possible way I can see to get across this huge open area and into the village is with an online assault. Machine guns and BARs will lead, followed closely by the rest of the platoon. I need everyone yelling, screaming, and running as fast as possible. Get your men briefed and wait for my order to charge."

Someone started to ask a question, "Are..."

Schultz quickly interrupted, "I could give a rat's ass what you think of the idea; go brief your men." Everyone left.

When the team leaders arrived, Mahan began to brief them on Schultz's plan. Before he finished saying "online assault," he was interrupted.

"He's fucking crazy. No one's ever ordered such a thing, let alone pulled it off. Hell, one machine gun alone could wipe out an entire squad," Cpl. Skaggs said.

"Shut the fuck up, Skaggs," yelled Mahan.

No one else said a word; they just stared at Skaggs.

"Machine guns and BARs up front; everyone yelling and moving double time," the corporal continued.

Within minutes of the last bomb explosion, someone screamed at the top of his lungs, "CHARGE! CHARGE!"

The entire platoon took off yelling and screaming. Machine gunners blasted rounds that pierced shrubs, trees, and huts. I felt like a madman on a suicide mission. I did my best to keep up with Mahan's pace, but my pack bouncing on my back caused me to fall head first, knocking off my helmet. My heart pounded so hard I could barely breathe.

Someone picked me up and shouted, "Bird, are you hit?"

"No, I don't think so!"

Cpl. West said, "Then move."

As soon as the lead marines stepped over the small wire fence, the VC (Viet Cong) soldiers fired their first shots. Machine guns, AK47s, and Chi-com grenades made everyone hit the deck. Still not over the fence, I could see Mahan a few yards ahead—no doubt wondering where I was.

Immediately screams sounded: "Corpsman Up, Corpsman Up!"

I quickly realized it was Whitmore yelling.

Mahan took off toward Whitmore's position to see who was hit. I worked my way over the fence and was soon with him.

It was Jackson. His body was ripped apart from machine gun fire. He lay face down, not moving, in a pool of expanding blood and softly mumbling, "Whit, I'm hit. Whit, I'm hit."

Whitmore and I tried to roll him over but quickly realized his insides wanted to fall out. I held them in but it didn't work. The bloody mess kept slipping over my hands onto the ground.

Whitmore yelled, "Where the hell is Doc?"

Jackson stopped breathing; he bled out. He was dead.

Mahan told Whitmore to get some help and move him down the trail to the Company CP. I sat back on my boots and slowly rubbed the warm sticky blood on my thighs. This wasn't the first marine I'd seen die, but Jackson was the first I felt attached to. Mahan tapped my helmet with the tip of his M16 and said, "We're moving out." He was on a mission to find the rest of his squad so he could assess casualties and report to Sgt. Schultz. The village was quiet except for an occasional shot or grenade exploding; marines cautiously cleared their objectives. The dusty red dirt trail was cluttered with branches from the air strikes, making maneuvering quickly difficult. Cpl. West was following me and for some reason kept clicking his M16 selector from semi to automatic, which drove me nuts. I tried to calm myself by listening to the chatter on the radio.

"First platoon reported another KIA," I told Mahan. He began to stride faster.

We came upon a woman with two small children. The three of us must have appeared haunting.

The small boy and the girl, who was not much older, were crying, and tightly clutching their mother's legs, one on each side.

The mother cried uncontrollably, while holding her hands in front of her face as if in prayer. On the ground in front of them lay a dead middle-aged man—no doubt her husband. My eyes slowly scanned the area looking for anything moving, anything suspicious. In the family hut, I saw a bamboo bed in the corner, a black pot smoldering on some rocks, and what looked like a dead chicken—their meal. I felt certain we were alone.

The mother cried and bowed in what appeared to be a plea for help; her children cried because they were scared and someone they loved was dead.

"You guys didn't see this," said Mahan, taking out his 45-caliber pistol.

BANG! The shot exploded the woman's face. Her body instantly dropped dead.

"Shit." My legs buckled, and I fell slightly backward. The children began screaming louder and louder. They turned in circles, terrified and confused. The boy placed his hands over his ears; the girl pulled tightly on her hair.

BANG! The girl's head blew apart; she tumbled backward, dead.

BANG! The headshot blew the small boy off his feet, causing him to land on his side, dead.

Mahan calmly returned his 45 to the holster. "Let's Go."

I couldn't move. I was mesmerized by the blood draining from the heads of the woman and her children. I found myself slowly walking away looking back at what I just witnessed.

What just happened?

Wasn't that murder?

I thought maybe there's something in the Rules of Engagement I had failed to understand and this was legal during war.

Confused, shocked, and unsure of what to do, I kept walking. *If he could kill them, he sure as hell could kill me.* I remained silent. Haunted, I couldn't stop shaking.

Their faces, their screams, and their pooling blood were frozen in my mind. I felt helpless, and I hated Mahan for what he did; yet, I had no clue what to do. All I knew was, as his radio operator, I must remain by his side—even though I didn't trust him.

Within a short time, the word was passed for everyone to dig in. Defensive positions were established inside and outside the village. Sgt. Schultz ordered positions to be set on a line from the fence we crossed when we first entered the trees, across the trail we had just walked, and ending next to a large ditch in the heart of the hamlet. First platoon continued the line from the ditch to the river, and third platoon set up in the open area we had charged across. The company command post took up a rear support position behind the three platoons.

That evening a chopper arrived to take out the wounded and five dead marines. When the medevac lifted off, I stopped digging. My bloody, sticky hands let the entrenching tool drop, and I sat back against the dirt watching the bird disappear. I thought of Jackson's southern drawl, his chew, his chatter— this fucking hell hole gave us just two weeks of friendship. It wasn't fair.

My thoughts were interrupted when Mahan returned and sat down with both legs dangling in the foxhole. He took his helmet off, laid it in my freshly dug red dirt, and lit a cigarette: "No Cs on the chopper, so no chow 'til tomorrow. It's gonna be a long night, but we're gonna kill some fucking gooks."

He looked at me and said, "Go get the team leaders."

"What about the radio?" I asked.

"Go get the goddamn team leaders!"

I jumped out of the foxhole and took off. I returned with Skaggs, Soliz, and Whitmore. Skaggs immediately started to ask about food. Mahan told him to "shut the fuck up," lit another cigarette, took several drags, and continued to stare at Skaggs. His eyes were packed with disgust. No one dared to say a word.

Mahan began the briefing. "At 9 p.m. artillery will begin blasting the far tip of the peninsula. I want two men per hole. Make sure the men know their fields of fire. Once these gooks start moving, they'll be on a dead run, so everyone stay alert. Spooky will be overhead dropping flares, which should keep the place lit, but I want everyone in their foxholes until sun up; any questions?"

I thought for sure Skaggs would say something. Maybe because he had been told to shut the fuck up so many times today, he didn't say shit. As soon as everyone left, I continued digging. Cpl. West helped, but Mahan left for what he said was a meeting with the Skipper, which I didn't believe. West and Mahan were tight, so I didn't say anything about the woman and her children, though I wanted to. Before long, Sgt. Schultz came by looking for Mahan, which confirmed my earlier suspicion because Schultz certainly would be at the so-called meeting. At 8:30 p.m., Mahan returned, jumped in the foxhole, and said, "Nice job, Bird. Think it's deep enough?"

"Hope so," I replied.

"We'll sure as shit find out," said Cpl. West. Mahan agreed.

We positioned all the gear in strategic locations so everyone could find things in the dark. Packs were outside the position in front and behind. The radio sat in the hole between Mahan and me.

Grenades and extra magazines lay next to the packs in front of each man. The only thing in the hole was the radio; which gave us plenty of opportunity to find an incoming grenade.

Company command called for a radio check at 8:58 p.m. I responded, "India two bravo, roger, radio check."

It was almost dark when I heard the drone of C-130 engines overhead; Spooky was on station. Mahan whispered, "Get ready, men; the artillery will be here soon." He no more than said it when in the distance I heard the sound of big artillery, BAH BOOM, BAH BOOM! Six guns fired together from two miles away sending 155-mm rounds weighing nearly one hundred pounds screaming down on targets two hundred yards in front of the company line. The explosions shook the ground, flashed darkness to light, and spewed shrapnel at a murderous pace.

"Whistles, do you hear whistles blowing?" I asked.

Mahan: "That's their signal to move. Pass the word to get ready."

West: "Get ready…pass it down."

Gunfire and exploding grenades were heard coming from first and second platoons' forward positions.

West: "I can't see shit."

Overhead a popping sound gave way for a flare to turn the darkness to light. Instantly, Mahan ripped a full burst from his M16, killing two VC ten feet left of the foxhole. The burst scared me so much I fell into West.

Mahan: "Shit, I never even heard the bastards."

Pushing me off, West said, "There!"

To the right front I could see ten or fifteen VC soldiers frantically running, crouching over, and carrying weapons. West and I started throwing grenades, while Mahan unloaded two magazines on automatic.

Some of the gooks fell dead, others changed direction and kept running. Skaggs' team opened up with a machine gun, more grenades landed near the scattering Viet Cong, and suddenly all movement stopped. Mahan quickly reloaded and ecstatically said, "I told you we'd kill some fucking gooks. Hot damn, guys. Good job."

The Viet Cong ran when the flares illuminated the darkness, and they froze in place as soon as they burned out. The waves of VC soldiers seemed to never end. As soon as another flare popped, the whistles blew, and the firing started. The entire village became a killing field cluttered with dead and dying enemy soldiers. Grenades blew body parts into trees. Some VC soldiers, fighting pain from their wounds, screamed for help. The crying and moaning became worse as more and more bodies piled up. Some screams were so close that Mahan randomly selected a body and ripped it with bursts from his M16 just to stop the noise.

At midnight, the skipper radioed for a status report. The report from third platoon was close combat, at times hand-to-hand. First platoon reported killing gooks who were trying to escape by swimming across the river. Sgt. Schultz reported his platoon "has several dead piled up and no report of casualties."

At sunrise most of the firing came to a halt except for an occasional shot from an M16—maybe a mercy kill designed to put some poor bastard out of his misery. Mahan climbed out of the foxhole, stretched, lit a cigarette, and yelled for the squad to be careful searching bodies: "They may be booby-trapped."

I hung my head on my forearms as I sat alone staring at the hundreds of shell casings and grenade pins littering the ground. I was trying to understand the events of the past forty-eight hours—not possible. Finally, I stood up and was immediately stunned by the number of dead bodies. I counted fourteen in front of our position and three more to the left. I had no idea the three of us killed that many. There was one I was sure I'd killed. In my mind, I could still see him running in a group of three when I shot him with a three-round burst.

I remembered hearing a surreal thud, seeing him spin to a fall, and slowly roll over. Mahan had yelled, "Hit him again." I put three or four more rounds into his body; he stopped moving.

Kneeling beside his body, I was surprised at how young he appeared. I stared at his open eyes and blood-soaked uniform. His helmet, shot full of holes, was tipped upright, and his AK47 was slung around his body. His pack was ripped apart from gunfire and rice was spilled from an old sock. He had no sandals; he was barefoot. *Could he have been washing his feet by the river when the artillery started or did he just start running out of fear, leaving his sandals behind?* It didn't matter. He was dead, and I'd killed him. I felt no remorse. I felt no guilt—just a sense of acceptance. It's an acceptance that comes only to those who have killed another human.

By noon the company had gathered one hundred and two dead bodies from the hardcore VC battalions R-20, V-25, and C-130. CH46 choppers arrived, hovering above nets piled with dead bodies; the corners were attached to a dangling cable with a large hook. As the birds lifted one net after another, arms and legs were hanging down from the nets as they slowly disappeared to an unknown location. I stared at the nets as they slowly faded out of sight and wondered where they would be dumped.

By noon the company realigned and started a search and destroy sweep of the village. Second squad moved up the trail we had entered on and passed the bodies of the murdered family. They were still lying in the same position, flies swarming around dried blood. Mahan glanced at them and quickly looked away, as if to say, "I wonder what happened to them?" I wanted in the worst way to tell someone, anyone, but still couldn't do it. When we passed the spot where Jackson died, I felt a sickening chill.

By the time the company reached the end of the peninsula, eighty-eight prisoners were captured without resistance. Some were found submerged in the river breathing through hollow reeds. The captured were made to walk single file connected with a rope looped twice around their necks and with their hands tied behind their backs.

Those who couldn't walk rode on tanks driven by ARVN (Army of the Republic Vietnam) troops who had arrived during the morning to provide the company added support. One badly wounded VC soldier who was riding kept crying for help, but the ARVN soldiers ignored his pleas. They kicked him and slapped him in an effort to make him stop, but he kept screaming. In the end, they pushed him off the front of the tank directly in line with the track, killing him instantly. Second squad walked beside the tank watching in disbelief as the mangled body was spit out the back. The ARVN troops laughed and laughed. Mahan said to me, "That'll teach that dumb bastard!" I didn't respond.

By mid-afternoon the prisoners were handed over to a marine unit from Da Nang, and India Company boarded trucks for the journey home. I took off my pack, sat back, and closed my eyes. The events of the past two days wouldn't stop spinning around in my mind. I thought about telling Lt. Saal what Mahan did as soon as we returned. I thought about the soldier with no sandals, Pfc. Jackson, the whistles, and the soldier crushed under the tank. But, most of all, I thought about the frightened woman, her children, and how they died. It all seemed like a bad dream.

Exhaustion, hunger, and frustration finally claimed my body, and I drifted off. When the truck stopped, we had arrived at the battalion base camp. I was home.

Mahan announced, "Company memorial service tomorrow at 8 a.m. Jackson was one of us. Be there."

I slowly shuffled my tired body back to the platoon area. When I entered the squad's tent, there was a new warm body sitting on Jackson's cot. He stood up as squad members stumbled by barely noticing him. I dropped my gear, looked at him, and said, "Where're you from?"

"Indiana, Sir."

"Some call me Bird. I'm from South Dakota."

"Should I take this cot, Bird?"

"Just as well, he's not coming back."

1st Lt. Fred Smith (Left) Captain
Henry Kolakowski 1967

Silver Star Medal with Combat V for Valor

Henry Kolakowksi, Jr.

Date of birth: July 13, 1938

Home of Record: Farmington, Michigan

Henry Kolakowski graduated from the U.S. Naval Academy at Annapolis, Class of 1961

Citation: "The President of the United States of America takes pleasure in presenting the Silver Star to Captain Henry Kolakowski, Jr. (MCSN: 0-81631), United States Marine Corps, for conspicuous gallantry and intrepidity while serving as Commanding Officer of Company I, Third Battalion, Fifth Marines, First Marine Division in connection with operations against insurgent communist (Viet Cong) forces in the Republic of Vietnam. On 30 January 1968, Captain Kolakowski's company landed by helicopter in the Hoa Vang District of Quang Nam Province and quickly established a blocking position to contain two Viet Cong battalions on a river island while a nearby Army of the Republic of Vietnam force prepared to assault the enemy position. When the attacking units encountered heavy resistance and faltered, Captain Kolakowski immediately effected the necessary coordination and led his company to relieve the attacking forces. The Viet Cong, well entrenched in a hamlet surrounded by wire entanglements and making effective use of excellent fields of fire afforded by open rice paddies, were successful in holding back the attacking forces by use of extremely heavy small-arms fire, grenades, and antitank rockets. With exceptional professional skill and courage, Captain Kolakowski reorganized his company while under the intense enemy fire, issued orders for supporting fire, and prepared the re-assault of the hamlet. Demonstrating superior tactical skill and inspiring leadership, he fearlessly exposed himself to the hostile fire as he led his troops in a second assault. When the lead elements of his unit succeeded in reaching the hamlet, he unhesitatingly advanced through heavy enemy cross fire and directed his men in aggressive attacks against the determined enemy. Consolidating his position with two platoons before darkness descended, Captain Kolakowski established a cordon by placing his remaining platoon in a blocking position adjacent to the Army of the Republic of Vietnam forces. Throughout the night, as the enemy repeatedly attempted to break through the perimeter in human wave attacks, he disregarded his own safety as he directed his men in maintaining their positions. The following morning, Captain Kolakowski resumed the attack on the entrapped enemy, contributing significantly to one hundred and two of the enemy confirmed killed, the capture of eighty-eight soldiers, and the destruction or confiscation of large quantities of ammunition, equipment, and valuable documents. By his exceptional professionalism, dauntless courage, and unswerving devotion to duty, Captain Kolakowski upheld the highest traditions of the Marine Corps and of the United States Naval Service.

CHAPTER EIGHT

"Courage meant overcoming fear and doing one's duty in the presence of danger, not being unafraid." —Eugene B. Sledge

I f Lt. Saal was in any way troubled, he certainly didn't show it as he began his briefing. As always, the patrol sounded simple. Depart the company position at Phuoc Tuong Pass by 9 a.m., target four checkpoints, and return late afternoon. The mission was to clear the area of any enemy activity escaping from Hue City (location of Tet Offensive major battle) by whatever means necessary. Second squad, led by Cpl. Skaggs, would take point; Lt. Saal and I would follow Skagg's squad. First squad was behind us, which left third squad to cover the rear. He closed the briefing with, "It will be hot and sultry and tough terrain, so take extra water. That's it. Go brief your men."

As the Lieutenant and I walked away, I thought 9 a.m. was perfect because by then the daily fog would have lifted. I hated fog because it made patrols spooky, causing guys to be jumpy. When marines get jumpy, shit always happens.

Life for me had changed dramatically during the past three weeks. Cpl. Larry Mahan, the murdering bastard, had rotated back to the states, removing a great deal of stress from my life. The battalion had been relocated farther north to a new base camp in Phu Bai. Lt. Saal's radioman had left the country after being wounded, and Sgt. Schultz recommended me for the position.

Along with more responsibility for me came a surprising promotion to Lance Corporal that Lt. Saal initiated. In addition, he trained me to read a map, control medevacs, and direct artillery—information I needed to help assure my survival.

Staging for patrol on Hill 90

Near 3 p.m. the platoon still wasn't at checkpoint two because of the extremely rugged terrain. Everyone was exhausted, thirsty, and frustrated with our progress, but there was no way to go, except forward. A call on my radio from India 6 (Captain Kolakowski) for India 2 (Lt. Saal) left me feeling Captain Ski was upset. After a brief conversation, Lt. Saal handed me back the receiver and said, "We're going up front!"

It appeared he was on a mission to find out what the hell was taking so long and why his entire thirty-seven-man platoon was strung out for over three hundred yards. When he reached the pointman Pfc. Doug Henson, Lt. Saal bolted past him on a dead run.

Henson asked, "Where in the hell is he going?"

I said, "Let's go."

I took out my 45-caliber pistol, cocked it, and together we followed him up the crest of the hill not knowing what to expect. Two other marines bolted past just as a huge explosion filled the air along with gray smoke and the familiar smell of cordite.

Someone yelled, "Corpsman Up, Corpsman Up!" Within minutes Doc Dixon raced past, while the remainder of the platoon dropped down and waited for word on the explosion. When I reached the summit, Lt. Saal was spread across a large flat boulder with his arms and legs in a pile of mangled flesh. Doc Dixon was rapidly trying to stop the bleeding and control shock. Suddenly without warning a "bouncing betty" (WWII landmine) popped out of the ground; someone had obviously stepped on it. The canister lifted three feet and dropped in a cloud of white smoke. As soon as it shot out of the ground, everyone hit the deck. I covered my head with my arms and waited for the blast. It was a dud. I couldn't believe it.

Within seconds everyone realized we were in a minefield. Lying totally still, I slowly moved my head in search of more metal prongs. They were everywhere. We were all too scared to move for fear of popping another mine, so everyone lay motionless.

Seconds went by, and Doc yelled, "Bird, get a chopper in here or Saal's not going to make it."

I thought, *Land a chopper in a minefield? You're out of your mind.*

Cautiously, I knelt up, and pulled my pack off to switch to the medevac frequency. It was then I heard a chopper flying high overhead, a Sikorsky CH34, flying south toward Da Nang. Not even trying to request a medevac through normal procedures, I immediately moved to an air frequency and started calling, "CH34 flying south between Phu Bia and Da Nang, do you copy, over." I repeated this several times then changed to another air frequency, repeating the same request.

Two CH34 chopper on LZ at An Loc 1968

After a couple tries I heard, "This is a CH34 on heading to Da Nang, over."

"This is India 2. I'm in need of an emergency medevac; can you assist?"

"I'm a mail bird. I have no gunners, but I will assist with calling for a medevac."

"Negative! Negative!" I said. "The emergency is my O1 (Second Lt.), and I need you to pitch your bird in any direction, so I can identify."

Instantly he turned right ninety degrees, and I quickly responded, "Hard right."

"Is the LZ secure?"

Without hesitation I responded, "Affirmative."

I told him to "turn on a heading of northeast fifty degrees" and when he was in range, I'd "pop smoke." (Popping a smoke grenade of green, yellow, or white gave pilots ground troop locations).

I threw a yellow smoke grenade into an open area, and he radioed, "I copy yellow."

I confirmed yellow, and he started his approach. I never once considered aborting the medevac because of no security or the minefield. I clearly understood Lt. Saal needed out or he would die within the hour.

2nd Lt. Tom Saal 1967

* * *

Over the years I've pondered how fortunate it was that a lone mail bird was flying above me at that exact time, how lucky I was to convince him to land, and how fortuitous it was that we were able to place Lt. Saal aboard a chopper without stepping on another mine. Some of the guys called it a miracle; others said it was just dumb luck. Regardless of what anyone said, I still believe it simply wasn't Lieutenant Saal's day to die.

The next time I saw Lt. Saal was in South Carolina at a battalion reunion some forty-one years later. He looked much the same other than, like all of us, he had aged. His physical stature hadn't changed, his manners were the same, and his voice gave me goosebumps. My biggest problem was I couldn't stop calling him "Lieutenant" even though he insisted I call him Tom. It felt disrespectful.

We spent several minutes discussing second platoon, the guys, and stuff we did in Vietnam. Then, in an awkward way he asked, "Do you know what happened the day I was hit?"

I was astounded. He had no idea. He said, "I only remember running up the hill and the explosion."

Struggling with my emotions, I unfolded the events of February 29, 1968, while he stared at me in disbelief.

I felt sorry he had lived all these years not knowing how he was wounded, not knowing about the minefield, and not knowing what happened to his platoon.

When I finished, he asked calmly, "So you saved my life?"

"No, Doc Dixon saved your life. All I did was land a chopper in a minefield to get your ass out."

He laughed, "I don't think so."

We hugged and then hugged again. As we stood there staring at one another I asked, "What the hell were you thinking when you charged up that hill?"

His response came without hesitation, "Captain Kolakowski told me if I wasn't at checkpoint two by 3 p.m., I was to turn around. It was 2:50 p.m., and I wasn't going to tell my exhausted platoon to turn around. I told myself *I would be* at checkpoint two on time."

With tears in his eyes, he said, "Captain Ski had told me Lieutenant Jack Ruggles, my best friend, had been killed the day before. Because of Jack, I too was ready to die."

It finally made sense to me; he simply did not care anymore.

* * *

When second platoon returned to Hill 90, darkness had filled the sky. I was physically exhausted. Mentally, the platoon was in shock, and no one except Lt. Saal had answers to all the questions. Captain Ski asked Doc Dixon and me for a debriefing, but neither of us could give him a definitive answer as to why Lt. Saal acted like he was on a suicide mission.

Doc said, "He will no doubt be dead on arrival in Da Nang."

Captain Ski was saddened by his report. At no time did the skipper question me regarding landing a chopper in a minefield without security, a clear breach of military procedure. I was certain I would be in deep shit, but, ironically, it proved beneficial to my future as a radio operator.

Gunnery Sergeant Harris arrived the next day from Phu Bia to take command of the platoon, so once again I had a new platoon commander. He ruled troops with a friendly but firm manner, kind of like a teddy bear of a drill instructor—if there is such a thing.

My time with Gunny Harris was cut short because Cpl. Jerry Bain was set to rotate home, and he had requested I take his place in the company command post. Captain Ski confirmed I was the man he wanted, and before I knew it, I was the senior radio operator for the company.

My responsibilities at nineteen years old were now greater than ever. The level of accountability, of dependability, and of commitment required were beyond anything I had ever imagined.

Lt. Saal indisputably prepared me for this day, and Jerry Bain knew it. He told me years later at a battalion reunion that Captain Ski requested me because of how controlled and competent I was under fire. He felt I could make quick decisions in critical situations, which gave me pause. I wonder if landing a mail bird in a minefield had anything to do with his decision. Regardless, I was proud to serve as his senior operator and accepted the responsibility gratefully.

Captain Henry Kolakowski, Jr., was one of the most highly respected, intelligent, and confident officers ever to command India Company. He graduated from the United States Naval Academy with the Class of 1961, and proudly wore his graduation ring every day—even in the bush.

His love, respect, and concern for the troops completely overshadowed any of his faults. He incessantly studied his map to confirm company locations because getting lost in dense mountain foliage, monsoon fog, and elephant grass six feet tall happened all too often for many officers. He made certain his officers understood where they were at all times and that they damned well better not lie about it. He always said, "If you're lost, tell me...don't let me find it out."

My duties as senior radio operator changed several aspects of my life—including only going to the bush when Captain Kolakowski was in command, which, to be realistic, was quite often. My other duty was command of the communications center, which operated twenty-four hours a day, seven days a week.

The radio room was set up in a large bunker with several radios located on an L-shaped work counter. Maps denoting the company's TAOR (Tactical Area of Responsibility) hung just above the counter so patrols and ambush sites could be easily pinpointed.

Two radio operators manned the station, rotating every six hours. Sleeping quarters in the bunker allowed for the OIC (officer in charge) to be readily available in the event of enemy encounters.

It was also the duty of the command center personnel to receive, sort, and deliver the mail whenever it was brought from Phu Bia or Da Nang either by ground or air. Sorting mail was always sort of fun, yet, at times, it was sad because some guys seldom, if ever, had mail. One marine in particular would show up every day to mail a letter, but not once during the time we occupied Hill 90 did he receive any mail. It wasn't uncommon to have mail delayed for days or even weeks, but for someone to receive no mail was strange. It breeds depression, which leads to anger, which results in marines with live ammo doing crazy shit like holding someone at gunpoint over the simplest of things. This happened one day when this same marine claimed Pfc. Binns stole his C-ration can of peaches. He was planning to kill him as a result. I can't for certain claim the lack of mail caused the guy to lose it, but I do know mail brought a whole new meaning to a miserable life. Captain Ski authorized an R&R for the guy following a request from his platoon commander.

It was during this time Sgt. Schultz rotated to the states, which was a sad day for me. He came to tell me he was leaving the next day and asked if there was anything he could do for me before he left. I asked him if it would be possible for him to visit my parents, and he assured me he would, for which I thanked him. He was a great platoon sergeant, and I was happy he made my life better even though he wouldn't take any credit. Several weeks later I received a letter explaining his time with my parents.

CHAPTER NINE

*"I believe that's the record high: 105.6." —
Navy Corpsman, First Hospital Company, Da
Nang, Vietnam*

When the battalion moved north to Phu Bia in February, I was amazed by the size of the base, by the airstrip, and by all the conveniences the base offered. It was as if I had moved off the farm and into the city. I experienced a hot shower for the first time in three months and, believe it or not, had laundry service. The squad tent was a huge improvement over what we had previously, and I actually received two warm cans of beer a week. More importantly, the Seabees (Naval Construction Unit) would trade anything related to the bush for booze, clothing, and just about anything one needed. I couldn't believe marines were actually stationed here for their entire tour.

My astonishment ended five days later when the company was dropped on a small LZ atop Hill 90 overlooking Phuoc Tuong Pass. It was the beginning of Operation Houston. Our objective was to keep a four-mile stretch of Highway 1 open for supply trucks traveling to base camps near the DMZ. Captain Ski organized daily squad patrols, night ambushes, and platoon sweeps to accomplish the mission. Considering the mountainous terrain, stopping small enemy units from imbedding mines in the road or ambushing a convoy was nearly impossible, but the challenge was met every day and night.

Looking southeast at Highway 1 by peninsula

Overlooking one of three critical terrain features in the battalion TAOR, Hill 90 was critical to keeping the highway open. Most important of the three was Hai Van Pass just outside of Da Nang because of its size and because it served as a fueling point. Phuoc Tuong Pass, closest to Phu Bia, was critical because of its location to battalion headquarters.

Lang Co Bridge located between the two passes was critical because if destroyed, the road would be shut down for weeks to rebuild the bridge. One company guarded the bridge, one covered Hai Van Pass, and India overlooked Phuoc Tuong Pass.

Hill 90 was established by the French with three distinct tiers; consequently, one platoon could occupy a single level. India's command post was located on tier three (the top) along with the second platoon, while first and third platoons held the other levels. A road ran from Highway 1 directly through each tier to the top. Hill 90 (named for its elevation) was the smallest in the area with the highest elevation being less than twelve hundred feet, giving the enemy a clear advantage when dropping mortars; therefore, bunkers were well fortified. Mortars became a daily occurrence, posing two problems: the mortars themselves and the number of huge rats living in our bunkers. The bunkers were the only source of protection from mortars, so living with rats became routine—especially at night.

Hill 90 looking east at valley filled with rice paddies
and French railroad track

Sometime near the end of March, I began to feel weak, had chills, and developed a slight fever. Doc thought I may have been infected by a rat because so many others had. As the days progressed, I continued to get worse and was put on a medevac headed to First Hospital Company in Da Nang.

Weakness made it nearly impossible for me to walk. By the time I was admitted to the hospital, my temperature was 105.6. I overheard a corpsman say, "I believe that's the record high." Before long I was diagnosed with p. falciparum malaria. Immediately, I was stripped nude and placed on a bed with a rubber mattress. A rubber blanket was placed over me and then connected to an air conditioning unit beside my bed. Within minutes I started shaking uncontrollably. After two hours my fever had broken, but I was too weak to eat, drink, or walk. I had almost a week of IVs before I was able to walk to the mess hall and actually eat solid food.

During one meal I recognized a marine I knew from staging battalion named Gunnery Sergeant Molleck. When I approached him, he immediately recognized me. He was in charge of graves registration and said that if I felt up to it,

I should stop over and spend some time with him. He said they were so busy during the Tet Offensive that literally rows of U.S. bodies were staged outside under tarps.

Several grave registration sites were located throughout Vietnam. Most of them were six-man, air-conditioned, metal units used to house bodies before transport to the main grave registration facility in either Da Nang or Saigon. Later that week I spent two days with Molleck fingerprinting, washing bodies, and taking personal effects inventory of marines killed in action. I quickly realized that working with the dead didn't bother me and started having thoughts about a future in the funeral service profession.

Interestingly, I also discovered why my M16 was covered in blood the first day I arrived in Vietnam. Drivers picking up "newbies" first stopped at First Hospital Company for supplies such as helmets, flak jackets, and M16s stockpiled from dead and wounded medevac'd marines.

After ten days in the hospital, I was discharged to full-duty status. I picked out a helmet and flak jacket, boarded a truck, and headed to the Da Nang airstrip. I caught a CH34 mail bird going to Phu Bia with a mail stop at Hill 90. I thought about asking if they, by chance, hauled a lieutenant's body to Da Nang on February 29th, but I decided I didn't want to know if Lt. Saal had died.

Author just after returning from hospital on Hill 90
French concrete fortification in background

When I returned, Captain Ski was eager to see me. He informed me that he had recommended me for the Vietnamese Cross of Gallantry (with a Bronze Star device), which I received several months later. The citation referenced several machine-gun positions I eliminated with artillery fire during Operation Houston. Years later I learned the award was given to soldiers, as well as Military Units, that served in Vietnam. The Government of South Vietnam awarded the medal for individual valor and considered the cross equivalent to our Bronze Star Medal.

The first marine division received one with a Gold Cluster and Gold Frame for its service during the war, thus I have two. Someone once said, "Medals are awarded to warriors to make them feel better about the atrocities they commit during war." On some level this statement may be true, but I've known individuals who chased medals constantly, namely my nemesis Cpl. Mahan.

General Patton once stated about the Medal of Honor, "I'd sell my immortal soul for that medal." Medals mean more to some soldiers than to others. My experiences tell me wartime medals and heroes are not produced; they just happen.

Vietnamese Cross of Gallantry with Bronze Star

Corporal Craig Tschetter

United States Marine Corps

Citation: "An excellent NCO, rich in the experiences of the battlefield and in commanding, always protecting the freedom of the Republic of Vietnam.

"During Operation HOUSTON, Corporal TSCHETTER, even though facing numerous numbers of Viet Cong, was very instrumental in the destruction of several VC machine-gun positions. As a result of his diligence and seemingly unlimited resourcefulness he gained the respect of all who observed him and through his outstanding leadership, professionalism, and loyal devotion to duty, he contributed remarkable merit to the glorious victory obtained."

CHAPTER TEN

"The core reality of war isn't that you might get killed out there. It's that you're guaranteed to lose your brothers." —*Unknown Vietnam Veteran*

P rivate First Class James R. Salisbury was born February 2, 1949, and grew up in Oregon. He enlisted right out of high school just as I had done, claiming he wanted to serve his country. Admittedly, I also wanted to be away from home. We confessed we missed our families but also acknowledged a belief in trying to help the people of South Vietnam. Our friendship began when the battalion moved to Phu Bia and he took the cot next to mine in the squad tent. I was never certain why he chose to be next to me, but whatever his reason, I was glad he did. When a care package arrived from home, we would both be excited because we always shared. Actually, we each took our favorites and then the rest was up for grabs. Moms knew to send canned items like SPAM, tuna, or Vienna sausage. My mother usually added a Big Hunk (long white nugget candy bar loaded with peanuts), which I loved but always split with Jim.

Pfc. James Salisbury (my friend)

Jim was, by my standards, a brave marine because he consistently volunteered to walk point. I hated point, but for Jim, it was where he said he needed to be. Point men are like corpsman and chopper pilots; they live in incredible danger that produces severe consequences. Jim said, "It comes with the turf—just like carrying a radio with a big antenna signaling *shoot me*." We made fun of the danger by saying it didn't mean anything anyway. Seriously not true.

Making jokes about being killed was common; levity diffused the thought of death. Once, as my ambush squad was getting ready to leave, Soliz said, "Hey Bird, tonight you get it in the head, bro." Everyone laughed, including me, but I thought about it more than I ever admitted.

LCpl. Larry Soliz with Cpl.
Richard Skaggs (in background)

On May 18th, the battalion was flown by chopper to Ga Noi Island to replace Third Battalion, Seventh Marines during Operation Allen Brook. Later, we attached to the Twenty-sixth Marines and fought the Thirty-sixth Regiment, Three Hundred and Eighth Battalion of the NVA for two weeks. By the end of May, marine casualties were one hundred and thirty-eight killed, six hundred and eighty-six wounded, and ninety medevac'd cases of heat exhaustion (the average temp was ninety-six degrees).

Ga Noi Island, located approximately twenty-five kilometers south of Da Nang, isn't really an island, but actually flat land surrounded by four rivers. When the rivers swell during the monsoon season, Ga Noi becomes an island. The hamlets, linked by hedges and concealed paths, provide a strong defensive network, making missions there extremely difficult. By the time we arrived, this one location had claimed more lives from our battalion than any other single location. It was home to the R-20, V-25 Viet Cong Battalions and the

T-3 Sapper Battalion (Special Forces). In addition, it was believed elements of the PAVN second division headquartered there.

One area was so dangerous that we called it Dodge City due to frequent ambushes and firefights. The terrain in Dodge City was much better suited for defensive forces than offensive, which made fighting there terrifying. I found my life dangling on edge each time I crossed a river onto Ga Noi in search of another enemy stronghold.

Ga Noi Island was considered the nucleus of a much larger place called the Arizona Territory, also serving as a sanctuary for several NVA units that were just as vicious as those on the island. It became home for the Fifth Marines for more than two years, and claimed more lives than Ga Noi Island. The Arizona Territory eventually took the being out of my soul and destroyed the one conviction I retained: trust of my own people.

Captain Ski found me in the communications tent and requested I get a solid head count as soon as possible. He knew the company was under strength, and a solid head count was important because tomorrow, June 9th, we were to depart for the Arizona Territory on Operation Mameluke Thrust.

Within the hour, I reported India Company strength at one hundred and thirty-seven marines, including officers, enlisted, and corpsmen.

"Are you sure?" he asked.

I could tell he was troubled by the count as he waved me off without saying another word. As I walked out of his tent, Lt. Ross was on his way in. "By the way, Bird, my count is two more bodies."

"If you tell Ski, it might make him feel better, sir," I replied.

By noon the next day, the company was airborne and heading to a base camp southwest of Liberty Bridge called An Hoa. Leaving Phu Bia was tough—no more hot showers or meals for who knows how long. I knew I would miss the shower most because it soothed my jungle rot and relieved the itching.

When the choppers circled An Hoa, it was clear this was not a small outpost, but a large compound with a huge airstrip. It wasn't as big as Phu Bia but definitely larger than An Loc and Hill 90 gave me some security. The number of tents and buildings appeared large enough to house several battalions.

Ski said, "There's over two thousand marines here, and this could be our home soon. Word is the Fifth Marine Regiment is moving out of Phu Bia. That's off the radar. You understand?" I assured him I did.

During the next three hours, tents were assigned, gear stowed, and everyone fed a hot meal at the huge mess hall. The guys found out we weren't leaving until morning so, as always, the party plans got underway.

The following morning's sunrise was silhouetted by weary soldiers (some, not all) staggering into the unknown. It was very quiet except for the sound of boots on the ground and an occasional clanging of gear.

My pack felt uncomfortable for some unknown reason, maybe because I didn't sleep much the night before, and I was humping extra gear. In fewer than three hours, we would cross the Song Tinh Yen River on to Football Island. I was filled with negative thoughts and not certain why; nothing felt right. Captain Ski, ten paces ahead of me, seemed different. He was usually calm, confident, and filled with a remarkable sense of command, but that was missing today. He had just returned from R&R in Hawaii with his wife, Linda. Maybe he was a little out of shape for the bush and knew it. Whatever it was, he wasn't talking about it, and I wasn't bringing it up.

The weather was hot and sticky, making my jungle rot flourish and weep pus. I used my sweaty neck towel to rub it away, but the salty sweat just made it burn.

Two clicks (two thousand meters) outside of An Hoa a sniper fired off a round, cracking the morning air. Everyone dropped to the ground.

"Corpsman up!"

Cpl. Carson (Company net radio operator) said, "Skipper, the point man (Pfc. Johnson) took a head shot; he's dead."

Cpl. Ron Carson 1968 south of Phu Bia

Ski requested to speak to the lead platoon commander; they discussed repositioning the platoon for an LZ. An hour passed before the medevac arrived, unnerving Ski all the more.

The downtime gave everyone needed rest, but by late afternoon, the heat was winning the battle. Word was passed to hold up. Ski called for the platoon commanders, and before long the company was digging in for the night.

The command post set up near a thicket, and I dropped my pack and flak jacket, giving my sweaty shirt access to the open air. I was relieved. When I decided to catch some sleep it was still so hot that I slept shirtless in just my flak jacket.

The next morning as I put on my shirt, I felt what I thought was a twig touching my bare back. I took off the shirt, shook it, and a 10-inch-long centipede as thick as my thumb fell out. It scared the crap out of me; Carson, Doc, Gunny, and Ski couldn't stop laughing.

The morning fog held us up for over two hours, but once we started moving, Ski ordered the lead platoon to pick up the pace. Yesterday's sniper was long forgotten when an explosion near the point platoon dropped everyone to the ground, which usually meant a booby trap. Time passed slowly. The radios went quiet. We sat waiting for word on what happened. Finally, Ski yelled at Carson, "Find out what the hell's going on."

Minutes later he reported, "The word is a booby trap, sir; no doubt an artillery shell. Two dead (Pfc. Lee and Weekley) and four wounded from India. They're looking for body parts, sir."

Ski's muffled voice said, "The merciless bastards won't stop."

The loss of his men was taking a personal toll; I had felt him becoming more frustrated each day. Captain Ski told me to alert Terrapin (call sign for battalion headquarters) of our situation and tell them we would keep them posted.

Carson yelled, "No emergencies, sir." Ski ordered me to put a hold on the medevac until all the body parts were found; he insisted they go out with the dead. I sat leaning on my pack wondering if every company commander would do the same. *Did other commanders think, to hell with body parts; we need to be at this objective by this certain time and just keep on moving?* I admired his commitment to his men as I stared at him sitting with his head in hands, elbows on his bent knees, patiently waiting for the words "All accounted for, sir."

Twenty minutes later Carson reverently said, "Sir, they're done."

Ski looked at me and said, "Call for the medevac."

"Yes, sir."

By nightfall we finally reached our objective. I let Terrapin know we were at the assigned checkpoint.

The next day, June 12, revealed something in the eyes of all the men that made me apprehensive—there was this rare sense of not being in control or maybe it was being completely out of control. Whatever it was, it was scary as hell, and it was not going away.

Within hours LCpl. Gentry was killed by a sniper's shot to the head. We had no clue where it came from. When Carson informed Captain Ski, his head dropped and he said to me, "Call a medevac."

By the evening of June 14th, the company had four killed, four wounded—and not once had we seen a gook. The company was angry, frustrated, and worn down: they were men looking for revenge. I kept sensing the worst and wishing Cpl. Hanley had never put those words in my head—"Marine, you *will* get hit. It's not a matter of *if* or *when*, it's a matter of just how *bad*." He was right, and I knew it.

At dusk Captain Ski and I talked about his time with his wife, Linda, which gave me a sense that maybe everything would be okay. Changing the subject, he said, "Oh, I forgot to mention—I promoted you to corporal before I left on R&R."

I didn't know what to say. Only a year ago I was a lowly private wondering if I would even become a marine, and now I was a corporal. I thanked him.

Before I fell asleep, I thought about him as a father to me and how important he was to my survival. I wondered if anyone called him Hank, like they did my dad, whose name was also Henry. He made me feel closer to my dad by being like the father I so wanted when I was growing up.

On day six our strength was down to one hundred and ten marines (KIA, WIA, heat exhaustion) and we moved just over five clicks from An Hoa. Ski's briefing with the officers was short. Second platoon would be on point (Pfc. Bruce King leading) following a wide trail along the river. Third platoon would run flank in the tree line, which left the CP and first platoon to cover the rear.

Shortly after dawn, the company was moving just as Ski ordered. Walking the trail behind him, I could see the river to my left. The river's bank was steep but comforting because I knew I had a place to dive if the unknown struck again.

During the late afternoon, Pfc. King spotted four uniformed NVA soldiers next to a small hut talking and eating their evening meal. They had no clue Bruce had them spotted. With revenge in his sights, he fired a burst from his M16, instantly killing two. The others disappeared into the tall grass and quickly returned fire hitting Pfc. King in the legs. Another cry for "Corpsman up" was sent back down the trail.

Immediately, second platoon became engaged in a firefight with NVA soldiers who had been lying in wait to ambush the lead squad. Carson quickly informed Captain Ski the lead squad was pinned down and alone on the trail.

Captain Ski said, "We're going up front."

Negotiating the trail was difficult. Small-arms fire hit the shrubs and dirt around us. Realizing we were being targeted, Ski dropped to the ground. Carson and I belly crawled up next to him. My radio went dead for some unknown reason. I quickly removed my pack and discovered a bullet shot through my pack into the radio. Ski quickly had us moving back down the trail where I replaced my radio with one from a passing squad radioman.

Ski radioed his lieutenants to slowly pull their men back to a more secure position, forming a one hundred and eighty-degree perimeter with the river to our back. "DIG IN."

I alerted the battalion commander, Lt. Col. Rexroad, of our situation; he ordered Ski to call him ASAP. Soon the company was in place. Ski requested I radio Terrapin 6 (call sign for Lt. Col. Rexroad). Captain Ski calmly informed him of the situation, the causality count, and the need to get the wounded out before dark. A quick glance at my watch told me it was nearly 6:30; I needed to get choppers here fast. Capt. Ski immediately ordered Cpl. Crane (artillery forward observer) to set up a fire mission. An Hoa was the nearest fire base, which Crane said was five to six clicks from gun to target.

Ski requested the first battery (six guns) to calibrate for three hundred yards in front of the perimeter; Crane confirmed. For each battery arriving thereafter, Ski directed they be dropped fifty yards closer. Finally, he requested that once the rounds are ready to fire *danger close* (within 50 yards), Carson should be told so he could alert everyone to get down.

Within minutes the perimeter was in place and the first six rounds whistled overhead, exploding at three hundred yards. Capt. Ski called for platoon commanders and 81-mm mortar forward observer (Larson) to the CP for a briefing. At the same time, Mike Wilson (Lt. Col. Rexroad's radioman) began to send me a shackle encryption over the radio about night assignments and the next day's mission.

Twenty minutes went by before Carson radioed, "Danger close, danger close, last rounds out."

He yelled to Ski, "Last rounds out, sir."

I could have sworn the prior two volleys weren't more than twenty feet above us. They scared the shit out of me. Immediately, I bent forward; I sucked my body as low to the earth as I could while continuing to decode Wilson's message.

Captain Ski, on one knee, continued to brief his team; his left foot was two feet away from my left shoulder. I faintly heard the guns fire in the distance, seconds passed, and then came a loud explosion with a rocketing of hurling steel. The explosion left me barely conscious, disoriented, and covered in dirt.

Am I hit?

I can't move.

What just happened?

I was in that zone of the unknown (a semi-conscious state of confusion, disorientation, and fear), with a loud ringing in my right ear.

Suddenly, the weight on top of me was gone; I looked up and saw the face of Doc Goss. I thought he was asking me if I was alright, but I could barely hear him speak.

"What happened?"

I thought he was saying, "Short round."

Still confused, I looked to my right and saw the smoldering impact crater just five feet away from me. The strong smell of cordite was burning my nostrils. The shrapnel must have gone over me. I couldn't believe I was alive.

Impact crater from short round on June 15, 1968
(blue X marks author's location)

Lt. Ross was a heap of torn dead flesh. Larson was unconscious and bleeding severely. Lt. Campbell was trying to stand up but couldn't find his balance; one arm was barely attached. Frantically, Doc Goss ripped Ski's clothes open, rolled him over, and lifted his limbs trying to find where he was hit. Ski fought desperately for air, flailing his arms and legs. I attempted to control his head, hoping to free his airway, but his thrashing prevented me.

Everything stopped.

Slowly his eyes rolled back, and he made two deep gurgles. Doc tried CPR for what seemed like forever. He quit, looked at me, and said, "He's dead."

Tears came quickly. I sat back on my boots while staring at his sweat-soaked, hairy chest and red dirt-soiled face. *Why do the good people die? Is there no justness? Why Captain Ski?*

Doc continued moving from body to body and then came back to me and said, "Are you sure you're okay? Can you hear?"

I stared at him as his hand wiped blood from my ear and neck: "You have a concussion."

At least an hour passed before I gained control of myself, confirmed the causalities, and contacted battalion.

Mike Wilson calmly answered his radio, "Terrapin, over."

"Terrapin, this is India," my voice trembled, "Stand by for a causality report, over."

Using my left ear, I revealed rank and last names (coded) of the casualties. When I came to O3 Kolakowski (KIA), Lt. Col. Rexroad got on the radio.

"India, this is Terrapin 6. I want you to know we're going to get help to you, but I need to know how many officers you have left, over."

"One WIA."

"I need to talk to him."

"He's being treated by a corpsman."

"What's the company's strength?"

"Maybe four cases of Coors."

"India, standby."

By the time I set up the LZ with strobe lights, I could hear the twin rotors of a CH46 medevac following the river to our location. I quickly moved back to a spot along the river bank with Pfc. Weber (Carson's replacement), so I could better direct the medevac. As the chopper turned to land, a door gunner opened fire with a 50-caliber machine gun. I shouted into my receiver, "ABORT, ABORT, ABORT!"

It was too late.

The machine-gun fire ignited a short-lived firefight between nervous marines. During the melee, Cpl. Crane was accidently shot dead. He had been acting as Lt. Campbell's radio operator. A short time later, I received word Lt. Campbell bled out from his wound and died.

Within two hours, India Company lost all of its officers, the company's gunnery sergeant, and two other marines, and several marines were wounded, including Cpl. Carson—all caused by our own people.

My thoughts were interrupted by Terrapin 6 on the radio. I informed him of our new situation. I couldn't tell if he was pissed or shocked. After a brief pause he said, "India, an officer will be inserted as soon as possible; you're doing a great job, son. Try to remain calm."

"Yes, sir."

Just then, Weber broke down crying and started to mumble, "We're going to die."

"That's not true," I assured him. Deep inside of me, though, I had never felt closer to death than I did at that moment.

Navy Cross

Campbell, Joseph Timothy

Lieutenant, U.S. Marine Corps (Reserve)

Company I, 3d Battalion, 5th Marines, 1st Marine Division (Rein.), FMF

Date of Action: June 15, 1968

Home Town: Stoneham, Massachusetts

Citation: "The Navy Cross is presented to Joseph Timothy Campbell, Lieutenant, U.S. Marine Corps (Reserve), for extraordinary heroism while serving as Executive Officer of Company I, Third Battalion, Fifth Marines, First Marine Division (Reinforced), Fleet Marine Force, in connection with operations in the Republic of Vietnam. On 15 June 1968 during Operation MARMALUKE THRUST in Quang Nam Province, Company I became heavily engaged with a large enemy force and sustained several casualties. As the company prepared to evacuate its wounded, an artillery round impacted nearby, killing the company commander, a platoon commander, and the company gunnery sergeant. Although seriously wounded by fragments, Lieutenant Campbell realized that he was his unit's only remaining officer and refused medical aid in order to assume command of the company. Despite his weakened condition due to the loss of blood, he ensured that a landing zone was secured and selflessly directed the evacuation of the other casualties. When the medical evacuation helicopter arrived and immediately came under intense enemy ground fire, Lieutenant Campbell fearlessly moved among his men to direct suppressive fire on the hostile positions, enabling the helicopter to extract the casualties. Ignoring his weakened condition, he directed a second helicopter into the zone to complete the emergency medical evacuation. He subsequently succumbed to his wounds before he could be evacuated. By his courage, inspiring leadership, and selfless devotion to duty despite the severity of his wounds, Lieutenant Campbell undoubtedly saved the lives of numerous Marines and upheld the highest traditions of the Marine Corps and of the United State Naval Service. He gallantly gave his life for his country."

Chapter Eleven

"Stay with me, God. The night is dark. The night is cold: my little spark of courage dies. The night is long; be with me, God, and make me strong." —*Junius, Vietnam Veteran*

"India, India, India, this is Terrapin, over."

"Terrapin, this is India."

"Stand by for Terrapin 6."

"India, this is Terrapin 6. A new captain is on a chopper heading your way and should be there shortly."

"I copy. A new skipper—that's good news."

"He's a good man. Hang in there, son."

Sometime after midnight Captain Jim Mitchell arrived, found his way to my location, placed his hand on my shoulder and said, "You've done a good job, Corporal. Are you okay?"

I thanked him and began unfolding the events of the day, trying not to cry, but I couldn't help it. I was weak with fear and sorrow. Capt. Mitchell claimed to understand and assured me everything would be fine.

The darkness made it hard for me to see his face, but he sounded competent and brave. I couldn't make out what was on his helmet, but I decided it was either a pack of smokes or a bandage stuck in his rubber helmet band. Regardless, he was here, and I was happy to have him.

"Let's go check the lines," he said. I told Weber to stay in place until we returned; he assured me he was not moving.

Pfc. Weber on Hill 90 1968

When the sun broke through in the morning, Mitchell was sitting across from me, legs bent up and studying his map. Stuck in his helmet was a red carnation. I couldn't believe it.

Why would an officer be in the bush with a goddamn red carnation in his helmet?

"Sir, what's with the flower?"

"Morale, Corporal—to boost morale."

I thought, *You've got to be shitting me; that'll piss guys off, not boost morale. He can't expect me to walk behind that moving target. He's going to get us both killed. What doesn't he understand?*

Two hours later, the remaining ninety-three men of India Company clearly understood the mission for the next two days. Kilo Company was close by and we had to link up with them to survive. Linkage required us to move forward down the same trail to the area we were shot out of yesterday. Cpl. Skaggs, who was now in command of second platoon, would be on point, followed by the CP, while third and first platoons covered the rear. Skaggs was ordered to stay on the main trail and move cautiously.

Before leaving, I took out my Kodak Instamatic 104 and shot a few pictures of the area: the shell crater, the ditch I'd laid in, the bandages littering the trail, and the guys sitting along the trail. For some reason, I felt a need to capture this location.

India Company troops on the morning of
June 16, 1968

Capt. Mitchell passed the word to move out, and India's shattered men started down the trail. I couldn't help but think about my buddy Salisbury walking point and how scared I would be if it were me. Knowing him, he was no doubt thinking about me having to follow a stupid red carnation. I figured we would have a great conversation about it when we got back to Phu Bia. *God, I wish we were there now.*

Before long, an explosion pierced the air behind us and immediately everyone was on the deck in firing positions. Word arrived that a booby trap seriously wounded LCpl. Miller. Miller was hurt bad. Doc didn't think he would make it, so Mitchell quickly had first and third platoons set up an LZ while I requested an emergency medevac.

Miller was unconscious but alive and, fortunately, the only one hit. Mitchell casually walked around like he was oblivious to danger. I thought, *Some sniper is going to blow a hole in that stupid carnation.*

"Where's that medevac?" Mitchell yelled.

"No word yet, sir."

I could tell he didn't care for my answer: Miller needed a hospital. Finally, I could hear the chopper and supporting gunship in the distance. Minutes later the medevac was on the ground, the Huey gunship circled overhead, and Miller was gone. To everyone's surprise, not a single shot was fired. Captain Mitchell slowly walked back to second platoon, greeting troops along the way. He was trying hard to keep everyone calm.

By late afternoon, the sun once again won the battle. Mitchell decided to set up night positions. A small, tight perimeter was put in place, and everyone, including me, began chowing down. Mitchell was plotting grids for night defensive fire called H&I (harassment/interdiction). He called the grid locations to the artillery battery in An Hoa.

They would start firing after dark and sporadically target grids. Our location was also given, so there was no chance of more men being killed because of a mistake like yesterday. I wanted to find out why that round fell short, but maybe some general had already covered it up.

"Tomorrow will be the ninth day since we left Phu Bia" was how I started my letter to Mom and Dad. I hadn't written a letter for quite some time—mostly because I didn't know what to say. If I told them about all that was happening around me, they would worry, and that was not fair. Part of me wanted to tell them everything so that they would realize how tough I have it, but I couldn't bring myself to do it. After all, I made the decision to be here—what a dumb decision.

If I'd listened to Uncle Ken, I wouldn't be in this hell hole. I wouldn't be scared out of my mind all the time, hungry, exhausted, plagued with rotting skin, and living in piss-soaked clothes. God, what was I thinking?

Without warning, a huge explosion shook the earth. "INCOMING! INCOMING!" Mitchell yelled, "Artillery." Incredibly, it was the only explosion, and more amazingly, Mitchell immediately knew why. He grabbed the radio, flipped the dials to the fire base frequency, and yelled, "Cease fire, cease fire!"

Instantly he was chewing someone's ass because they admitted putting our grid location in the gun for the H/I target.

Mitchell was furious and swore someone would be busted for the mistake. Luckily, no one got hit, but twice now we had been targeted by the same people. I told myself the whole operation was cursed. I felt certain I was going to die; I knew it.

In the morning, Mitchell was on a charge. He briefed the squad leaders, rotated platoon locations, and within the hour we were moving. Kilo Company along with H&S Company was within clear striking distance, and he intended to link up today. Our movement went unobstructed the entire day; however, Kilo and H&S were pinned down by sniper fire and couldn't move. There would be no linkage today. Mitchell was content with setting up a night perimeter and giving the troops some rest. I was too.

The next morning seemed to come quickly, but I felt rested and ready to find our sister company. Mitchell called the squad leaders together for a briefing and pointed to a large tree line in the distance.

"That, men, will be where we find Kilo Company," he said. Everyone stared at the trees on the horizon and puzzled looks slowly appeared on all faces. It wasn't the tree line that was the problem; it was the open stretch of rice paddies we had to cross to get there. Mitchell said, "First platoon's turn to be up front, CP will follow, then second and third."

It didn't take first platoon long to reach the rice paddies and suddenly come to a stop. Questions were passed back to Mitchell about where to cross to find Kilo Company.

Mitchell moved forward, and I followed. He pointed to a location straight across, stating it was the fastest and safest. Kilo would be at the far end of the trees off to the right.

Everyone understood, and first platoon started the walk across the narrow paddy dikes, moving vertically and horizontally as if on a checkerboard while they moved closer to the tree line. The rest of the company followed on the same path, slowly stretching out into the open.

Twenty yards away from the tree line, the gooks opened fire on the lead squad. They hit us with machine guns and small-arms fire from several locations. There was no place to move; we were pinned down behind two-foot dirt dikes and paddies filled with water and rice plants. Machine gun fire continued to ping the dikes' dirt, causing men to crawl quickly in one direction or the other to find cover.

Lying in the water on his back beside me, Mitchell contacted Terrapin and requested air strikes to silence the machine guns so we could try to pull back. He was certain we were close enough that the shrapnel would go over us and we would just have to deal with the blast wave.

"If we don't get out of here, we're going to lose a lot of men," Mitchell said.

"No shit, sir!"

He had Weber pass the word to the platoon leaders to hold fast until the air arrived and then we would start pulling back.

It seemed like forever before the first sortie arrived, but once the first six bombs landed, the firing stopped. The concussion blast felt warm as it passed, causing my right ear to begin ringing. Mitchell ordered everyone to move back after the second bombing run and to keep moving unless shots were fired. The second sortie soon ended, sending shrapnel zinging overhead. Everyone took off running. The bombs worked. Within minutes the entire company pulled clear and safely hunkered down in a cemetery filled with large grass mounds.

For close to an hour, sortie after sortie, pounded the tree line. I kept wondering, *How could anyone survive after being pounded by that many bombs and napalm?*

I took pictures of the planes, napalm, and bombs falling. I thought that maybe someday I would want to look at them.

Captain Mitchell once again called a meeting of the platoon leaders. Everyone knew where we were going, but not a single person, including me, wanted to cross those paddies again. When Mitchell started to explain the crossing, Cpl. Skaggs immediately volunteered second platoon to go first. He no more than finished, when Jim Salisbury said, "I'll take point." He was one brave marine—far braver than I. He looked at me, and I shook my head in disbelief.

Minutes later Jim was leading the company across the open paddies as if nothing had ever happened. The closer he got to the tree line, the more nervous I felt. A quick count put me eight men from the front because Captain Mitchell wanted to follow the lead squad. I told myself, *This is where I think they opened up last time, but, so far, nothing.* Everyone was on edge, expecting the worst to break loose, but this time there was no gunfire.

Jim entered the battered tree line stepping over fallen trees while continuing to move forward. Suddenly, he stopped, dropped to one knee, and passed the word back: "The trail goes both ways, which way should I go?"

Mitchell forgot to tell him Kilo would be to our right, so he passed the word up to go right. Jim was quickly up and moving to the right on the trail as ordered. More and more of us rushed to enter the trees. Mitchell held Weber and me up while he directed troops to various locations. Just a short distance from us was a large bomb crater, and Mitchell told Weber and me to wait there for him.

"This is one spooky place," I told Weber as we slid into the crater. He commented on the smoke and fallen trees. Mitchell joined us, continued to direct men down the trail and others farther into the trees, and reminded them to stay spread out.

CRACK! One gunshot was heard.

An eerie sense of silence overtook everyone as we waited. My heart began pounding. Seconds later Skaggs came running back down the trail to Captain Mitchell and said, "Salisbury's hit; he's my man, and I want to go get him." Mitchell hesitated to consider Skaggs' request, then nodded his head. Skaggs abruptly turned and hunkered over, then ran up the trail.

We waited.

We waited longer.

"CRACK!"

Another single AK47 shot.

One after another, marines ran back down the trail, and jumped in the crater.

"Both Salisbury and Skaggs are down," someone said.

"It's got to be a spider hole," another said nearly out of breath.

Immediately, Mitchell threw his helmet down, pointed at two machine gunners and said, "You two come with me."

To me, he said, "Stay here."

Away they went with machine guns blasting the ground and shrubs on both sides of the trail.

Minutes passed. There was an occasional machine gun burst, and then I saw Mitchell running toward me with both hands behind him gripping Jim's boots. Jim's head was bouncing on the dirt trail like a car tire on a ribbed road. Mitchell quickly turned, flipping Jim into the crater. His dead body tumbled to the bottom in a twisted ball of arms and legs. Not far behind, the two machine gunners dragged Skaggs' dead body to the edge of the crater.

I stared at Skaggs and then Jim. I couldn't stop shaking. I felt like I was falling apart. I hated this fucking place. Seconds later, everyone heard the familiar sound of a mortar leaving its tube: THOOOP!

Someone yelled, "Incoming!"

We all covered our heads awaiting the explosion. The mortar landed just outside the crater, and immediately Weber yelled, "I'm hit!"

When I looked up, he was rubbing his arm and laughing, almost uncontrollably: "It's my third heart; I'm going home. Bird, I'm going home!"

What a lucky shit; wounded three times and never once seriously enough for evacuation. Meanwhile, Jim got hit one time, and he was dead. *Where's the justness?*

Mitchell contacted Kilo 6 and was informed they were less than a click away and would hold their position until we arrived. I had already called for a medevac, which would take Jim and Skaggs to First Hospital Company in Da Nang.

Their gear would be thrown on piles; their bodies would be delivered to Molleck's team. *Maybe I should put a note for Molleck in Jim's pocket telling him he's my friend. Hell, Molleck might not even be there—and he would probably care less.*

Weber quickly asked Captain Mitchell if he could go out on the chopper. "No, we will be at An Hoa in a few days." Weber wasn't happy, but Mitchell didn't know about Weber's other hearts. Plus, the only one who cared was Weber.

We spent the afternoon sweeping the tree line, destroying everything that remotely looked NVA. Guys yelled, "Fire in the hole" as they dropped grenades into bunkers and spider holes hoping to kill someone.

Dead bodies lay scattered from the bombing, while others charred black from napalm lay smoldering. I shot some pictures wishing one of these dead bastards was the one who killed Jim. At that moment, I hated them so much I would have given almost anything to kill one.

By late afternoon, Kilo Company fired a green flare marking their position. Kilo's commander and good friend of Captain Kolakowski, First Lt. Fred Smith, greeted Captain Mitchell with a slight smile. He, too, looked exhausted, and I could tell he was sad about Ski. It's not what anyone would have considered a reunion setting, but we were sure happy to finally be united. Smith and Mitchell began talking about the past few days and where we needed to be before dark when I heard laughter.

I slowly walked in that direction. Six guys were standing in a circle around an NVA soldier who was severely wounded and near death. His belly was split open, exposing his insides; his legs were split open and disfigured. His eyes were fixated on the blue sky.

It was obvious he wanted to die because he tried to choke himself on dirt. He gagged and coughed up blood, bringing laughter to his audience. Frustrated, he placed his weak hands on his intestines and pulled them to the ground.

Someone said, "This dumb shit can't even die."

Seconds later, Sanchez's boot slid a splinter of wood from a tree to the NVA's hand; he picked it up. Weakly, he tried stabbing his gut, wanting desperately to die, but his body continued to breathe. Finally, someone shot him in the head either out of anger or mercy—maybe both. I turned around and slowly walked away, my vengeance satisfied for what these bastards did to my friend Jim.

Someone said, "Good job, Bird." I felt no guilt, no remorse.

Several days later while walking at the tail end of Kilo Company, we entered the perimeter at An Hoa. It was the same perimeter we left some weeks before.

The toll on India Company was obvious to all who remained, but for me the losses were devastating. I was shattered, and Captain Mitchell understood why. He was solemnly sympathetic to my losses; I was grateful to him.

India Company needed to rebuild in order to be an effective fighting force, and Lt. Col. Rexroad understood that clearly. Consequently, on July 5th, twenty-six days after we left Phu Bia, we returned to our home base. Just thirty three badly beaten-down marines walked off the choppers at Phu Bia that day.

CHAPTER TWELVE

"I hate war as only a soldier who has lived it can, only as one who has seen its brutality, its futility, its stupidity." —*Dwight D. Eisenhower*

From a distance I could see Gunny Caleb patiently rolling the end of his handlebar mustache and leaning against the doorframe of India Company's office. I felt certain he was scanning the area for signs of company personnel or, should I say, what was left of it. He no doubt received word the company was scheduled to return to Phu Bia today. I suspected he was most interested in seeing anyone from the Command Post to discuss what happened on June 15. When I finally got within range of his gravelly voice, he said, "Jesus Christ, Bird, we heard you were dead." I dropped my forty-pound pack by the office steps, sat down, and assured him I was not dead—yet. Others from the office gathered around with surprised looks, and for over an hour, I reviewed the events of the past few weeks. It was very emotional for me, but I realized they longed to hear from someone who was there, not just rumors. After all, Captain Ski and the other officers were a big part of Gunny's life as the acting first sergeant.

The conversation quickly ended with the arrival of Captain Mitchell, who had told me on the LZ he would meet me at the company office. Mitchell was quick to speak. "Gunny, I want you to find some steaks and beer. We need a company gathering tonight. These men have earned their down time and some good chow. Pass the word as soon as possible."

"Yes, sir, will do."

Then Mitchell looked at me and said, "Corporal, get some rest. We'll see you tonight."

He turned to leave, looked back, and asked, "Gunny, which tent is mine?"

I suddenly realized he'd be a stranger in a tent that was once the home of officers who were now dead. I remembered the newbie when I returned to Jackson's empty cot several months ago. Gunny quickly said he'd walk him over and that they had already cleared the area of the other officers' personal effects. As they left, I returned to the communications tent, found my cot, and crashed.

Gunny did a great job in setting up an area in front of the company office for the cookout. By the time I arrived, things were well underway. Guys were busy drinking, smoking cigarettes, and bullshitting about every topic possible. The smell of steaks cooking filled the air as I opened a cold beer for the first time in weeks. Gunny had found some ice, too.

Weber seemed the most excited because Gunny had assured him he was going home. I was happy for him—but also jealous. Guys kept telling me the word was I was being recommended for a medal—possibly a Silver Star for my actions on the day Ski was killed. I didn't have much to say because I was still overcome with loss. Some very special people in my life were gone. I was angry and hurt. I tried to act unchanged, but my mind was telling me something else. I kept feeling I might be falling apart, and I didn't want any sign of weakness to show. I told myself I needed to suck it up and move on—but this was different. I was in more pain than I thought possible.

July brought fresh troops, new relationships, and time to heal from June's impact on the company. While other companies in the battalion were involved in Operation Houston Phase IV, India Company stood down for twenty-one days.

It was during this time I was granted R&R to Bangkok, Thailand, for seven days. It proved to be the best thing for me emotionally. It healed my soul. I thanked Captain Mitchell more than once. It had been his idea to get me out of country for a break.

When I returned, I felt mentally refreshed and physically rested. I hoped I had the strength I needed to see my December rotation date. In addition, the daily hot baths had cleared up my jungle rot, making me feel even better.

Prior to leaving Bangkok, three guys failed to make the flight and were AWOL (absent without leave), punishable by court martial. One of them was an officer, so it turned into the main topic of conversation flying back to Da Nang. Other topics discussed were, of course, personal experiences, how much money we had spent, and how much food we had consumed. The excitement slowly dwindled the farther we flew. Finally, the plane landed in Da Nang, and the magical experience came to an abrupt end.

During the last week of July, the Fifth Marine Regiment moved headquarters from Phu Bia to An Hoa—just as Captain Ski had told me the day we arrived there to launch Operation Mameluke Thrust in June.

For Mike Company and India Company, the move required little effort because on July 26th, the two companies went OPCON (Operational Control) to the Seventh Marines, providing support for Operation Mameluke Thrust.

On August 6th, Captain Mitchell was replaced with First Lt. A. M. Clements, making him my third CO in less than two months. First Lt. Clements was a seasoned officer having commanded Lima Company and most recently serving as Battalion S-2 officer (intelligence). I felt a tremendous loss when Mitchell left because he gave me so much in terms of mental support. Before he departed he told me, "First Lieutenant Clements is a short-term replacement. A new captain will be in command within less than a month. Hang in there, Corporal; you're a good marine."

* * *

The next time I saw Captain Mitchell was in 2004 at a battalion reunion in La Grange, Georgia. I hadn't remembered him being so tall, but I clearly recognized his voice. He, like all of us, had aged. He had become an attorney in the state of Maine.

Captain Jim Mitchell with wife Libby in
La Grange, Ga. 2004

When we met, he said to his wife, "This is the radio operator I was telling you about before we came. Libby, this is Craig Tschetter."

He obviously hadn't mentioned the red carnation because when I brought it up, she said, "My God, Jim, what were you thinking?"

He sort of chuckled and tried to explain his reasoning and she kept saying, "I can't believe you would do such a thing. This poor young man must have felt terrified."

I tried to change the subject, but Lt. Col. Rexroad joined us and greeted the newly arrived couple. Jim's wife innocently said, "We were just talking about the red carnation Jim wore into the field when Craig first met him."

The colonel looked at Jim and said, "What! You did what? I don't remember seeing a flower that night."

I could sense Captain Mitchell was getting uncomfortable and, no doubt, felt embarrassed, but now Rexroad knew. To confirm the story, which I'm certain he didn't believe, Rexroad excused himself and went to confer with his own radio operator Mike Wilson. Rexroad asked Mike if he remembered anything different about Captain Mitchell the night he had sent him to India Company when Captain Ski was killed.

Without hesitation Mike said, "Well, he had a red flower in his helmet band; is that what you mean?"

Rexroad couldn't believe it. I think he actually thought I was lying because no officer under his command would ever do something so stupid. I later told Mike Wilson that for years I had thought it was a dream or some sort of fantasy. I thanked him for confirming my memory.

He said, "Rexroad was shocked when I said a red flower." We laughed about the stupid things that happen and how years later the stories surface to amaze us all.

* * *

The Arizona Territory (Valley) was located two clicks northwest of An Hoa across the Song Thu Bon River. Its boundaries consisted of two rivers and a chain of mountains that drifted into Laos. The Ho Chi Minh Trail flowed directly into the Arizona, which then fed troops to Ga Noi Island located due east and the Arizona Basin to the southeast. For all practical and tactical purposes, the An Hoa base camp was completely surrounded by hostile terrain filled with seasoned NVA units and NVA-supported Viet Cong groups. Some estimates claimed as high as 80 percent of VC forces were North Vietnamese Army personnel. Marine companies would spend weeks at a time in the mountains, Arizona Territory/Basin, or

Ga Noi Island, and each time they returned, they looked like the walking dead.

Not only was the area around An Hoa filled with seasoned NVA but also a massive number of booby traps, ranging in size from a hand grenade to two hundred and fifty-pound bombs. From the lowland rice paddies to the high mountain ridges, heavily fortified positions lined the landscape. There were spider holes, deep trenches, and a highly sophisticated underground tunnel system. During one patrol we discovered a tunnel system complete with a hospital operating room, boxes of surgical instruments, cooking/dining areas, and sleeping quarters for thirty men.

From March through August the sun relentlessly beat down on our heavily packed bodies, leaving legs to ache and feet to burn in pain. Sleep was non-existent; instead, short semi-consciousness was about all one could expect.

Week after week and month after month of walking paddy dikes and trails left me promising myself I would never walk anywhere again my entire life.

The constant worry of booby traps, sudden gunfire, or incoming mortars pushed my mind to the limit, creating anger, frustration, and fatigue. After a couple weeks in the bush, it would come to an end with a short two-day break in the rear.

Yet, by late 1968, the An Hoa base was a constant target of rockets fired from random locations in the surrounding mountains. Like the sound of a mortar leaving its tube, the sound of a rocket being fired quickly registered in my mind. Some days five or six rockets hit inside the perimeter, making the once safe respite an even greater hazard than the bush. Life quickly became more and more dangerous. I was plagued with thoughts of my not leaving the hell hole alive. My rotation date was December 13, and as far as I was concerned, that day couldn't come soon enough.

CHAPTER THIRTEEN

"There were no rear lines to escape to, there was no escape from the stress of combat, and the psychological stress of continuously existing at "the front" took an enormous, if delayed, toll." —*Anonymous*

September brought not only a change of seasons, but also a new company commander by the name of Captain M. A. Gurrola. Short, burly, square-chinned, and covered in black hair, he quickly became known by the guys as Captain Gorilla. Personally, I found my fourth commanding officer gentle—but all marine. He excelled in no nonsense, respect of command, and demanded excellence from officers as well as NCOs. He expected corpsmen to do their job: save lives and care for his men. As for me, he requested I keep him informed of battalion matters and remain close at hand at all times, especially under fire. He let everyone know where they stood on the day he joined the company in the field at Ga Noi Island on September 2, 1968.

Normally, the monsoon season began during late September or early October. During most years the cold, wet, windy weather was gone by late February. However, 1968 wasn't a normal year. On September 5, Typhoon Bess came ashore and created three days of havoc. The battalion raced to escape the swelling rivers around Ga Noi Island just in time to reach the safety of Liberty Bridge Base Camp. It was my first experience in a typhoon but, by no means, the last. The cold rain and torturing wind made life miserable for everyone, but for those of us in the bush, it was a time of being perpetually soaked. The only warmth was from urine freely pissed down one's leg.

During the first week of October, I received a surprise letter from someone I hadn't thought about for a long time.

When we did receive mail, it usually came in bundles because of the time between the bush and a base camp. Occasionally, mail was delivered to the bush, but the bright red mail bags were more of a burden than they were worth.

I had a habit of organizing my mail in chronological order and by person. Usually, I would read Mom's mail first because sometimes she sent pictures, followed by letters from my siblings, and then whoever else.

This strange letter, however, I read at the very beginning. The return address read Della Nordaker, Virgil, South Dakota. *Why was she writing me? And how did she know I was in Vietnam?*

It turned out she and her mother, while visiting my aunt Marie, were informed of my location, and Marie asked Della if she would write me a letter. Somewhat surprised by the request, she decided to say, "I do remember Craig, so sure I'll write him."

Every letter of Della's thereafter I read first, and sometimes I had three or four to read before I would get to Mom's. God, I looked forward to her mail and couldn't wait until the day I might actually get to see her. I needed to get out of this place alive before that was going to happen, but seeing Della sure was exciting to think about.

During the afternoon of October 5th, the Battalion CO alerted Captain Gurrola the battalion was on standby for an operation called Maui Peak. Two NVA regiments and a rocket regiment surrounded an Army Special Forces camp at Thuong Duc. Two of the compound's outposts had been overrun, and the enemy was seriously threatening the main compound. Several marine and army units were put on standby for a potential insertion around the threatened compound.

Della 1970

The next morning at 10:30, we received word of an insertion. The company boarded choppers and departed for LZ Sparrow located four kilometers south of the Special Forces camp.

The Command Group was in the fifth bird scheduled to land, which as a short-timer made me feel good. For three hours prior, the LZ had been pounded with two hundred and fifty-pound bombs to ensure a safe insertion. As the first two choppers attempted to touch down, they were targets of heavy machine-gun fire, forcing everyone to abort. Unable to safely land, the choppers returned to An Hoa and waited for new orders. Within hours we lifted off for another helicopter-assault, only this time on LZ Kiwi, nine clicks northeast of LZ Sparrow. Safely landed, we moved north a click and set up a position overlooking the Song Vu Gia River. At dawn on October 7th, we moved into the rugged mountains to begin a steep climb to reach LZ Sparrow. Casualties mounted daily from falls and heat exhaustion because of the steep vertical slope. At times my face was barely a foot away from the mountain's slope.

On the second day, we lost eight marines to heat exhaustion and maybe advanced one hundred meters. Finally on the foggy morning of the 14th, we walked on to LZ Sparrow. A cool, wet, eerie feeling met the company as they cautiously came off the slope into the open.

The sound of mortars leaving their tubes sent everyone running for cover. I found a large boulder with enough room for me to slide under, with Captain Gurrola squeezing in tightly as well. Fortunately, no one was hit, but we moved through the LZ in a big hurry and continued to climb.

Tropical Storm Elaine struck later in the day and began dumping rain that lasted for seven days, bringing war to an abrupt halt. India Company clung to the steep mountain slope for five days without food or resupplies. Reluctantly, Captain Gurrola authorized the opening of packages from families of the marines no longer with us, so food could be shared. The poor marines selected to carry the mail bags were quite pleased to unload those packages.

A total of thirty-nine inches of rain fell, and thirteen inches came on one day, making it almost impossible to keep from sliding down the slope. Holding onto shrubs and bracing our boots against exposed roots saved us but produced severe cramping. Relieving ourselves was nearly impossible because troops were strung out all across the mountainside.

On the eighteenth, we were ordered to move down the slope to a new location for extraction. The pouring rain made descending extremely dangerous and produced slips and tumbles down the mountain. By the end of the day, the entire company was off the slope and slowly moving to our extraction grid.

Dai Hiep 3, a small hamlet on the southern bank of the Vu Gia River, is where we set up for the night on October 19th. Captain Gurrola placed the CP under a roofed hut in order to keep the radios dry—plus I think he was ready to be out of the rain. The only corpsman we had left stayed in the CP, but Gurrola made him go check each man for immersion foot. He was not happy.

At 1:00 a.m., a Sapper Unit (NVA Special Forces) attacked the perimeter by simultaneously landing grenades in each perimeter foxhole. The night erupted with small-arms fire, grenade explosions, and screams from wounded marines. Within seconds, sappers were running freely inside the perimeter, firing AK47s and lobbing grenades as they ran through the village from one end to the other. It reminded me of the Alamo back in January—only this time they were coming from every direction.

Word started arriving on the company radio net of the dead and severely wounded, along with requests for a medevac. Captain Gurrola was busy plotting artillery grids for outside the perimeter, when everything stopped. The firing ended… everyone waited…nothing happened…they were gone.

Gurrola whispered to me, "Get some choppers in here."

He gave me our grid location, and I quickly placed the request. Just then a marine completely out of breath crashed to the ground in the CP and said, "The artillery team is dead; direct hit by a grenade in their foxhole, and there's lots of wounded, sir."

Gurrola sent him back with orders to spread the word that we only had one corpsman, so everyone should do the best he could; medevacs were on the way.

He handed me the map with the artillery grids and told me to order a fire mission on the first three. He took the company radioman (Reynolds) and left to check the perimeter. He returned just as the locals were starting to surface from underground shelters. Gurrola yelled, "Di di mau, di di mau," which meant "Move now, move now." They quickly disappeared. I think they heard the artillery—not Gurrola.

Several tense minutes passed before the first chopper checked in with me on the radio. I told Gurrola, "Birds are on final approach, sir."

He immediately called for a cease fire on the artillery.

I moved down to the LZ located in the paddies just outside the hamlet. A small perimeter comprised of a few marines and two strobe lights inside overturned helmets served as the LZ. The pilots could easily see the lights from above. I directed them to land between the strobes. We had five KIA and twenty-three WIA, and several were emergencies; Doc got the emergencies on first.

After the next chopper landed and departed, I noticed Doc was gone, so I radioed the pilot who said, "He's on board."

After loading the next chopper, I returned to the CP to inform Captain Gurrola of what the pilot told me. He was furious. "That's desertion in the face of the enemy," he kept saying. "I'm going to court-martial that son of a bitch."

I told him the count at the LZ. He hung his head and waved me off to return to the LZ.

What took place next has always been a question for me. I remember moving quickly back to the LZ when an explosion knocked me off my feet, throwing me into some shrubs and leaving me in that *zone of the unknown*. I lay there for several minutes afraid to move. I could feel my body felt intact, but my head was pounding like someone hit me with a sledgehammer. I could feel blood draining from my right ear onto my neck.

I lay there quietly for more than an hour, not sure what to do—remain, get up, or crawl away. *Was it a sapper or a marine that caused the explosion?* I rolled over and began feeling the ground for my helmet. I couldn't find it. Finally, I cautiously crawled toward the CP and eventually stood up and walked. Being inside the perimeter I felt reasonably safe, but very uncertain about what happened. Captain Gurrola and Reynolds spotted me, and knowing something was wrong, both rushed to my aid. I was trying to explain what happened when Gurrola grabbed Reynold's radio and alerted the platoon commanders of possible sappers still inside the perimeter. The more information I shared, the more he thought it was a local villager's homemade concussion grenade. It made sense because there was no shrapnel, just a huge explosion.

"Where's your helmet?" Gurrola asked.

"I don't know," I replied.

"We'll find it," he assured me.

The entire incident went unrecorded primarily because the only corpsman we had was gone, and Captain Gurrola ended up having him court-martialed. He never returned to the company.

Several years after my discharge, I decided to make a formal request through a Veterans Administration Service Office for three medals I never received although they were listed on my discharge papers. When the box arrived, it contained the three I ordered plus, to my surprise, a second Purple Heart. Captain Gurrola must have reported the incident requesting a Purple Heart, which I had never claimed because it was never recorded on my discharge records.

Operation Maui Peak officially ended on October 20, 1968. The marine casualty count was twenty-eight KIA and one hundred and thirty-eight WIA. NVA losses were two hundred and twelve. The Army Special Forces camp resumed operation soon thereafter but continued to be a target of attack for several months.

Chapter Fourteen

"Short-timer, in the Marine Corps, usually meant
less than 30 days before one's rotation date."
—*Marine Jargon*

By the end of October, I started to notice the concerns of being a *short-timer*. So many things had happened during the past year, and the thought of remaining alive until my rotation date (December 13) caused mind games. My twentieth birthday was coming up on November 22nd, and I really did want to see age twenty. Unfortunately, the daily surroundings and activities left it easy to become fatalistic, making life even more uncertain. I didn't want to harbor a defeatist attitude, but the uncertainty of life can be a powerful head game.

First Sgt. Colby stopped me on the way back from the mess hall and said, "Stop by the company office. Your orders arrived this morning." *My orders—shit; now I know I'm short.* I didn't even go to my tent; instead I sat on the company office steps and waited for Top Colby to return.

When he finally arrived, he handed me my orders to read. I looked at them and said, "I don't understand what they say."

"How in the hell were you a radio operator for so long," he snapped. "You're going to Sea School in San Diego to become a Military Police Officer on a naval vessel. You get to guard the goddamn Navy."

I couldn't believe it.

"I don't want to be on a ship," I said.

"Well, that's where you're going, marine, so get that shit out of your head," he replied.

I took the orders and walked back to my tent totally discouraged that the Marine Corps would place me on a ship. Hours of frustration passed before I went to Captain Gurrola with my new orders. He tried to help me understand the importance of marines on naval ships, but I still disagreed. Then out of the blue he said, "Well, I'll make you a sergeant if you come back for another tour, and as a sergeant, you will be able to pick your next duty station."

I thought, *Another tour...you must be crazy.*

He said, "Think about it for a few days, and we'll talk when we get back from the bush." His parting words were, "It's only seven months, not thirteen."

For India Company, Operation Henderson Hill lasted a few days, and within one day of returning from the bush, the entire battalion was ordered back to the same area under a new operational name called Operation Meade River. There was just enough time for dry clothes, a hot meal, and a short rest.

Captain Gurrola informed me Cpl. Reynolds would take my place, and as policy required, I was to stay in the rear until my rotation date. I was outside the policy's two-week window, but I had taken him up on his offer to return for the seven-month tour, which may have fueled his decision. Part of my agreeing to his offer was confirming his word that I would not be in the bush when I returned; he agreed. I chose my thirty days of leave in South Dakota even though I could have picked anywhere in the world.

My family played a big role in my decision, but I also had a real desire to see Della Nordaker. She promised me that if I would come to South Dakota State University in Brookings, she would go out with me, even though she was dating someone else at the time.

On November 17th, a rumor quickly passed through An Hoa that a squad from the Twenty-sixth Marines had been overrun on an ambush and executed by the NVA. Each soldier was shot in the back of the head as they knelt on the ground. The story scared the crap out of everyone, but it was quickly passed off as a rumor. The next day, however, confirmation came; seven marines from the Twenty-sixth Marines had been executed.

On November 20th, Top received word a CH46 chopper was shot down and crashed into India Company's Command Group. The chopper instantly burst into flames killing everyone on board and engulfed Captain Gurrola and numerous others in flames. Although he suffered severe pain and couldn't lower his arms, he refused to be evacuated until all the others were treated and sent to First Hospital Company in Da Nang. His actions were duly recognized, and he was awarded a Silver Star several months later.

On November 28th, Top sent me to Da Nang to deliver his mail before I departed for home. Captain Gurrola appeared happy to see me, shared the accident story, and told me one of the passengers killed was Mike Company's commander. The accident bothered him, and he told me he was grateful I wasn't with him at the time. I wished him well and left for home.

The day I left Vietnam I had mixed emotions—not about leaving, but about the decision I had made to return. I knew two other guys that made the same decision, but they loved the thrill of killing. Most thought I was crazy or simply hungry to make rank. Either way I had made the decision, and now I had to live with it.

I spent two nights in Da Nang at the transition area and actually slept on a mattress each night. I drank more than I should have the first night but was ready to fly out on the morning of the third day.

The Pan American flight was packed with loud, overjoyed soldiers. The environment couldn't have been more jubilant, and the voices were full with the spirit of having survived.

When the pilot throttled up the engines and the plane's nose lifted, the men erupted in cheers of joy. Several promptly provided the country with a single finger salute and loved every second of it.

I sat there acting just like everyone else—clapping and giving high-fives. Yet, inside me I was struggling, knowing I was a phony. Sure, I was going home, but I didn't want anyone to know I was coming back to this hell hole. *Who in his right mind would choose to roll the dice with death for seven more months?*

Silver Star

Michael A. Gurrola

Action Date: November 20, 1968

Service: Marine Corps

Rank: Captain

Home of Record: San Diego, California

Citation: "The President of the United States of America takes pleasure in presenting the Silver Star to Captain Michael A. Gurrola (MCSN: 0-86269), United States Marine Corps, for conspicuous gallantry and intrepidity in action while serving as Commanding Officer of Company I, Third Battalion, Fifth Marines, FIRST Marine Division, during combat operations against the enemy in the Republic of Vietnam. On 20 November 1968, during Operation MEADE RIVER, Captain Gurrola and his company were heli-lifted into an area in Quang Nam Province where a large friendly force was to assemble in preparation for an aggressive assault against hostile units. After he disembarked and was establishing control and coordination of the assault elements, one of the helicopters crashed into the command post and burst into flames, which engulfed Captain Gurrola and his command group, causing numerous casualties. Although suffering extreme pain and unable to lower his arms to his sides, Captain Gurrola steadfastly refused medical evacuation and, for the following five hours, calmly directed the efforts of rescue teams while simultaneously controlling and coordinating the movements of the uninjured members of the assault force. Ignoring the danger of enemy small-arms fire and the possibility of further injury from exploding ammunition and fuel aboard the aircraft, he refused to relinquish his command until all the casualties had been evacuated and a complete report had been rendered to higher headquarters. His heroic and timely actions inspired all who observed him and undoubtedly saved the lives of several Marines. By his courage, steadfast leadership, and unwavering devotion to duty in the face of grave personal danger, Captain Gurrola contributed significantly to the accomplishment of his unit's mission and upheld the highest traditions of the Marine Corps and United States Naval Service."

CHAPTER FIFTEEN

"It's a funny thing coming home. Nothing changes. Everything looks the same, feels the same, even smells the same. You realize what's changed is you." —*F. Scott Fitzgerald*

The final leg of my flight home was two hours from Denver to Sioux Falls on Western Airlines. It was a solemn two hours of reflection about Vietnam with intermittent thoughts of family, a new car, and home-cooked food. I had made up my mind I wasn't going to cry when I met my family. I planned to remain strong even though I knew my mother would be a mess.

Several months ago I had asked my father to order a new Plymouth GTX with the muscle 440-cubic-inch engine and four-speed transmission. I wanted it just like the picture in the car magazine I was reading at the time—a green exterior, black vinyl top with black interior, and bucket seats, of course. I had over a thousand dollars to put down on the four thousand, seven hundred-dollar car, and felt certain I had earned it.

As the plane taxied to a stop in front of the Joe Foss Field Terminal, I could see my family standing outside the door. A lump suddenly appeared in my throat and my eyes began to water. A young stewardess walking by asked, "Are you alright?"

I assured her I would be fine, just a little nervous.

"Are you returning from Vietnam?" she asked.

"Yes," I replied.

"Well, welcome home."

I was smartly dressed in my Marine Corps green wool uniform with matching cover and shined shoes as I departed down the steps from the plane.

Mother was standing up front with a huge smile and waving open arms. When we met, she couldn't stop hugging and kissing me. Surprisingly, it was my father crying tears of joy, while my sister and two brothers stared in admiration. They continued hugging me until we embarrassingly realized we were blocking the entrance.

Wow! It felt so good to be home after thirteen months. I couldn't believe it. I felt we had so much to talk about, yet I had so little I wanted to tell them. Part of me wanted to tell them story after story about what I had lived through, the friends I lost, the miserable conditions I lived in, but in the end, I decided not to. They wouldn't understand anyway. How could they? If they knew what I had truly experienced, what might they think of me? More importantly, I wasn't certain how to tell them I was going back to Vietnam. I felt like I was betraying them, which left me feeling unworthy of their unconditional love. I knew how devastated they would be. They had prayed for my safe return every day and now I was about to put them in agony once again.

Mom was still holding my hand when she slid in the front seat beside Dad. Everyone else piled in the back. Her perfume smelled of lilacs, her touch as soft as ever; I could tell she was relieved beyond belief. I felt blessed to be sitting beside her warm, loving self. Somewhere outside of Sioux Falls, Dad asked, "What's your next duty station, son?"

Being an old Navy guy, he knew I had a four-year hitch, so I obviously would be stationed somewhere. Mom was stilling gently rubbing the top of my hand when I announced, "I'm going back to Vietnam."

Instantly, mom twitched and covered her face with her hands as she burst into tears. She couldn't stop crying and kept repeating, "No, no, no. No more."

I felt terrible. The car went quiet except for Mom's distressed cry. I had all I could do not to cry, so I stared out the window, knowing I had just broken their hearts again.

Minutes later I said, "What do we know about the car, Dad?"

He responded, "It's at the dealership."

"How can you talk about a car?" Mom said with disgust. Then she hugged my arm and laid her head on my left shoulder.

"Will you be safe?" she asked.

"Yes, I'll be in a secure base camp—a long way from the bush."

"How long will you be gone?"

"Seven months, and then I'll be stationed in the states," I replied.

She slowly started to rub the top of my hand again, giving me a sense of peace and comfort.

After a couple of days everything seemed normal, and I felt they accepted my decision to return to Vietnam. I wasn't surprised that they didn't ask many questions, but one night Mom mentioned Sgt. Schultz's visit. She actually forgot his name but said he was so nice and such an honest man. She also wanted me to know that God works in mysterious ways and that it was God's plan we were together in Vietnam. I assured her I thought she must be right.

What I didn't tell her was Schultz had written me a letter telling me about his experience with my family. He said that after he left the house, he drove two blocks, pulled over, and cried his heart out. He lied to them so much it broke his heart. He wrote, "I just couldn't tell those lovely people the danger you were in, so I told one lie after another."

Later that night I couldn't help but chuckle about Mom's comments. If she only knew the real Sgt. Schultz, there would be no question in her mind that he was destined for hell. Schultz was a crusty marine sergeant who loved to shoot the village pigs (less food for the enemy) and carried an M79 grenade launcher. One day an NVA soldier carrying a machine gun (who had us pinned down) got up and began running outside a tree line when Schultz stood up, fired and hit him with an M79 round. He exploded into a thousand pieces, which filled us with laughter and cheers.

He admitted later it was a lucky shot, but it sure made the guys feel good. My mother saw him as a nice, honest man; I will always remember him for his willingness to help me, his bravery, and his hard-ass demeanor.

During my second week home, I drove to Brookings to see Della Nordaker. I arranged a meeting through some old friends who were married and going to South Dakota State University.

They knew Della and allowed me to stay with them at their apartment in married student housing. Della was living in a dorm at the time.

I told the lady at the desk inside the dorm entrance I was there for Della Nordaker. She curtly ordered me to have a seat while she called her room. A short time passed and then off to my right, I saw her coming down a set of wide steps dressed in an orange knit dress cut just above mid-thigh. She was the most beautiful sight I'd ever seen. I couldn't believe she was coming to see me. I was overcome. How I could be so fortunate as to go out with such a beautiful woman amazed me. We picked up my married friends and went to dinner at the Town House. I was absolutely elated to be with Della and my friends and in a safe, clean, and healthy environment.

I saw her one more time during those thirty days—New Year's Eve when she was home from college for the holidays. Her father cleared snow for hours from their quarter-mile-long driveway and part of the county road just so I could pick her up. I decided he either liked me or wanted his daughter to enjoy New Year's Eve somewhere other than at home. What's most interesting about the two times we shared together in December 1968 is that I never once kissed her. I respected her so much; I didn't want to destroy a future with the woman I adored.

CHAPTER SIXTEEN

"Until a warrior had three missions he shouldn't open his mouth; after five missions he could be relied upon to tell a war story honestly; ten made him a seasoned warrior; fifteen and he was running out of luck; twenty and it was hard to explain why he was still alive." —*Studies & Observation Group saying*

Sitting on the Pan American flight from Okinawa to Da Nang, I was wondering if I might be the only soldier going back to Vietnam. I was also wondering if my luck could hold for another seven months. I was pushing the odds, and I knew it. Captain Gurrola convincing me to return was suddenly starting to haunt me. Deep in thought, I glanced out the window into the night sky and there, looking at me, was my reflection. Staring at my image, I realized that I alone had made the decision. I was the one, not Gurrola, who placed this potential death sentence on my life. I quietly said, "Don't blame him, you idiot." *My God, what was I thinking when I made the decision to come back?*

My thoughts were interrupted by the marine next to me asking, "Have you been to Vietnam before?"

"Yes."

"Is it true the area up by the DMZ is the worst place to be stationed?"

I turned from the window, looked him in the eyes and said, "It's not going to make a damn bit of difference where you're stationed. You can get killed anywhere at any time."

He never said another word. I laid my head against the window and continued staring into the darkness.

Thoughts of home and my time with Della kept being interrupted by thoughts of An Hoa and who might have been killed while I was home. I thought about First Sergeant Colby and what he would assign me to do for the next seven months. I wondered how many rockets were hitting the base each day and where the company was operating. Then I thought of Captain Gurrola lying in the hospital and wondered where he might be. My mind kept racing back and forth until finally my eyes turned heavy, and I drifted off with memories of home.

Hours passed before I heard the pilot say, "Gentlemen, we will be landing in Da Nang in approximately one hour. Let me be the first to thank you for your service to our country. We wish you all the very best and look forward to your return flight. Thank you, again. Stewardess, prepare the cabin for landing."

The sun was up and so was everyone on the plane. The noise level rose dramatically. I unbuttoned my shirt pocket and took out four three-by-five cards my father had given me before I left. He had written the words to an old gospel hymn on them for me to carry as a reminder of God's love and strength. It must have been hard for him knowing I was a troubled believer; regardless, I accepted them with appreciation. The hymn was written in 1865, at the end of the Civil War—no doubt to give comfort to returning soldiers. I read the words and re-read them several times before we landed. I tried to imagine how Dad felt or what he might have been thinking when he copied the words to that gospel hymn, "Day by Day."

Top Colby was having another bad day when I arrived at the company office in An Hoa to begin my duties as a member of the rear echelon, as Captain Gurrola had promised. Top looked up from his desk and asked, "Where the hell have you been?"

I swear to God he was tougher than a woodpecker's lips and meaner than hell. I tried to explain I was held up at

Treasure Island Naval Base over a misunderstanding with my orders when he interrupted me and said, "I don't give a shit about TI. As far as I'm concerned you're over two weeks late, and in my Marine Corps, that would be called AWOL. Captain Gurrola needs a radio operator, and you're just the guy I need to send him."

Within hours I was in the bush on Operation Taylor Common operating in the Arizona Territory high up in the mountains. Captain Gurrola acted surprised to see me jump off the chopper and was curious why Top sent me. After I explained the trouble with my orders and about Top calling me AWOL, he seemed to understand why I was there. Unfortunately for me, it didn't make one bit of difference. The conversation was over.

Operation Taylor Common began on December 6th and lasted until March 8th. The thrust of the operation was to clear the NVA from a well-known stronghold called Base Area 112 located in the mountains adjacent to the Arizona Territory.

Once the marines had established artillery fire bases in the mountains, the lower An Hoa Basin area would begin being cleared of well-entrenched NVA troops. India Company along with other elements of Task Force Yankee occupied Combat Operations Base Javelin. Operational command was given to Colonel Michael M. Sparks of the Third Marine Division, who had recently moved his battalion to An Hoa. Within two weeks of taking command, he along with his staff were killed when their chopper was shot down by machine-gun fire near Fire Base Maxwell. I could tell it bothered Captain Gurrola— maybe because of his experience on Operation Meade River.

For me, the time spent in the bush was cut short after Captain Gurrola decided in early February that we would leave the bush together. He was scheduled to rotate on February 15th, and he felt a need to fulfill his promise to me. A new captain named Bieler would be commanding India Company, and Gurrola made the decision we'd served enough time in the bush. I was not going to argue with his decision. We boarded a chopper in the Arizona Territory and returned to An Hoa. It was February 13, 1969: one of the happiest days of my life.

Operation Taylor Common lasted until March 8, 1969, with marine losses of one hundred and eighty-three KIA and just under fifteen hundred WIA. NVA losses totaled nearly fourteen hundred KIA, along with twenty-nine captured.

CHAPTER SEVENTEEN

"To write is human, to get mail: Divine!"
—*Susan Lendroth*

Top Colby made the decision to move the company office underground the day after a rocket slammed into a tent near the office and killing four marines. The Navy Seabees took almost two weeks to complete the project, but once done, everyone felt much safer. The bunker design called for thick wooden beams covered by sheets of metal and stacked with four feet of sandbags. The Seabees guaranteed a direct rocket hit would not collapse the structure; however, no one cared to find out. Electricity was from a small generator providing adequate lighting and power for Top's coffee pot, a hot plate, and electric typewriters. The walls, floor, and ceiling were wood with a wide wooden stairway ascending to the outside. Scented candles helped reduce the musty smell, but controlling insects like cockroaches and other creatures was not possible.

The bunker served us well as both a work environment and sleeping quarters; however, I preferred to sleep outside on top of the bunker, as did others. The loud siren denoting incoming rockets gave us plenty of time to race down the stairs to safety. Of course, it helped to be sober, so you could find your way out from under your mosquito net. An Hoa certainly wasn't the same as Khe Sanh, but I gained a greater appreciation for the Twenty-sixth Marines stationed there during the Tet Offensive of 1968.

In addition to office duties assigned by Top, I served as sergeant of the guard on Delta Section of the perimeter. I was required to sleep in a command bunker with radio operators and with the OIC (officer in charge) for that week. I had my own jeep, with driver, and was responsible for checking the bunkers on the perimeter throughout the night.

If there was an attack in Delta sector, I, along with the OIC, were required to oversee the security of that section of the perimeter. Making certain everyone was awake required approaching the bunker in total darkness until you heard someone in the bunker yell, "Who goes there?"

I would announce my presence with, "The sergeant of the guard."

If everything worked well, they would complete a sentence with the proper password to which I responded with a sentence verifying the password. For instance, if the password was spider, they might say, "We found a large spider in our bunker tonight." I might respond, "I had a pet spider once." I would then approach the bunker and check to be certain they were okay or find out if they needed food or coffee, which I always had in the jeep. At no time did I know for certain that they were alone and not held captive, nor was I certain that they wouldn't, for some reason, just start firing at me out of fear or start firing at me because they were hopped up on drugs.

Sergeant of the Guard duty usually came around every three weeks, and I absolutely didn't care for it because drug use was really starting to be a problem. I heard later that from 1969 to 1973 drug use continued to rise, leading to homicides, suicides, and death from drug overdoses. Race issues also started to surface around that same time. Neither of those issues were present during 1967–'68—at least not in the Fifth Marine Battalion where I served.

On February 24, 1969, the An Hoa ammo storage area (dump) was hit by NVA sappers, and the entire ammo dump went up in one huge explosion after another. The amount of live artillery rounds, grenades, and ammunition launched from the dump into the An Hoa Base Camp was incredible. Delta Section was located close to the ammo dump, and fortunately for me, I was not on duty as sergeant of the guard for Delta Section that day.

Top Colby ordered Cpl. Doug Henson (who was in the rear to rotate home) to form a squad and move near the exploding dump to engage the sappers. Doug said to Top Colby, "I'm going home in two days."

Top didn't care. I looked at Doug and told Top Colby I would take the patrol as a sergeant, and Top reluctantly conceded. Doug was extremely grateful, but Top was worried about losing one of his office staff.

As the patrol moved cautiously toward the exploding ammo dump, live artillery was whistling over our heads to land and explode some distance away. At one point a dud round landed directly beside us and stuck in the ground without exploding. It made me think of my experience one year earlier with Lt. Saal and the dud Bouncing Betty.

Small-arms rounds cooked off like Fourth of July fireworks, zipping by and at times cracking near our heads. Fortunately no one got hit. At no time did we encounter sappers, and by morning light, I moved the squad back to the company area. Doug was happy to see us return unscathed.

* * *

I didn't see Doug Henson until 2004 at a battalion reunion in La Grange, Georgia. During the course of our conversation he thanked me for taking the patrol on the night the ammo dump blew up in 1969. I remembered the patrol, but I had forgotten I volunteered to replace Doug. He sincerely thanked me again for what I did to protect his short time left in Vietnam.

* * *

Reading material was hard to come by, but an occasional *Playboy* surfaced in the office and was, of course, read from cover to cover. The one thing we could count on was the *Stars and Stripes* newspaper, which came weekly. It too was read from front to back, and we always had plenty of copies.

The first thing I always read was the KIA listing from across the country covering all branches of the service. The other area I would read was a small section of requests for information regarding the death of a certain individual.

In April, 1969, I spotted a request regarding "information about the death of their son Pfc. James Salisbury KIA on June 18, 1968, Quang Nam Province, USMC. Respond to: Mr. Earl Salisbury, Lebanon, Oregon (parents)."

For several days I pondered whether I should write them, and if I did, what I should tell them. Finally, I decided to write a letter of introduction with the understanding that I was a friend of Jim's, that I was with him when he was killed, and that I would be willing to share what happened if they requested I do so. Parents of marines killed in action received a form letter from the Marine Corps stating their son or daughter died as the result of "enemy small-arms fire" or an "enemy exploding device." Never was a family given details of how their son died other than those two descriptions. I decided I would first write to see if they really wanted more detailed information or whether they simply wanted to make contact with someone who knew their son.

A few weeks later I received a letter postmarked Earl Salisbury, Lebanon, Oregon. While I was reading the letter, I was overjoyed. They thanked me for befriending their son and asked me "to please, by all means, tell us what happened to Jim." So on May 20, 1969, I composed a two-page letter detailing the events of June 18, 1968. I started the letter with "Dear Friends."

* * *

On March 9, 2006, I received an email from a marine I served with in Vietnam named Robert Wunderlich. Bob informed me his work with the federal government took him to California recently for an inspection of a nuclear facility, and while on the tour, he noticed a gentleman's name was Skaggs. He mentioned he served in Vietnam with a marine named Skaggs. The gentleman replied, "My cousin was a marine and was killed in June of 1968."

Bob asked, "Was his name Richard?"

"Yes."

"I knew him. We served in the same company."

"His two sisters live near here. Would you like their phone numbers?"

"Yes, I would like to invite them to dinner," replied Bob.

The three of them met two nights later for dinner and had a long conversation about the brother they called Dicky. They had all sorts of questions, and Bob openly admitted he served with their brother, but only for a short time before being sent off to language school. However, he told them that there is someone he knew named Craig Tschetter who would be able to answer all of their questions because he was there the day Richard (Dicky) died.

Kathy, one of the sisters, immediately asked, "How does he spell his name?"

Bob said, "It's pronounced 'cheddar,' like cheddar cheese, but its spelled T-s-c-h-e-t-t-e-r."

"I have a copy of a letter written to the Salisbury family several years ago from someone by that name," she replied.

After reading Bob's email, I called Kathy in California, and we visited for a short time. I asked her for a copy of my 1969 letter to the Salisburys, and she assured me she would email a copy of the letter as soon as she got home. Later that evening I received the letter I wrote Jim's parents dated May 20, 1969, from An Hoa, Vietnam.

I read the letter several times even though it contained poor sentences, misspelled words, and the partial truth about the day's events. For Jim's family, it must have meant the world because they contacted the Skaggs family and then drove to California to meet them and provide a copy of my letter. I've often reflected on Bob Wunderlich meeting a cousin by the name of Skaggs and how I now have in my possession the letter I wrote to my best friend's family forty-eight years ago. I read it twice as I wrote this chapter, and I'm still amazed.

* * *

Life for me during the few remaining months in Vietnam was pretty mundane except for an occasional race-related altercation among the troops from the bush and the rear. Animosity was growing between bush marines and a number of colored marines (the term of acceptable use in the 1960s, according to the NAACP). Some (of color) always seemed to find a way to avoid the bush. It was called *skating*, and it didn't sit well within the ranks. On one occasion there was an actual race riot that ended with a colored marine telling me: "When I get out of the Corps, I will find your ass and kill you, mark my word, you piece of shit."

I suppose it didn't help that I hit him in the face with the butt of my M16 and knocked him down the steps of the company office bunker, where he was being held prisoner for drug possession.

When the day came for me to finally leave, I was ready and eager to depart Vietnam once and for all.

On July 27, 1969, I boarded a CH46 chopper in An Hoa and told myself I never wanted to return to this God-forsaken country.

My orders were to report to Drill Instructors School in San Diego, California, during the third week of August. As a sergeant I could request my next duty station, so I put in for Embassy Duty, Recruiter Duty, or Drill Instructor School.

I was certain I would never be selected for DI School knowing only the top 10 percent of marines qualified, according to Top Colby. When my orders arrived he said, "There's got to be a mistake; they selected you for DI School." I'm not certain he ever gave me credit or a compliment the entire time we served together. Regardless, I still considered it a privilege to have served under his command.

This time, the flight out of Vietnam was for real. I didn't have to fake my feelings or regret what I had done. I was going home and was as happy as I had ever felt in my life. I had rolled the dice with death long enough and considered myself fortunate to be alive. I was ready to go home.

CHAPTER EIGHTEEN

"The Marine Drill Instructor: They will admire him and they will fear him. When it's all over they will remember him for the rest of their lives." —*USMC Quote*

Class number 2-70 of the United States Marine Corps Drill Instructor School in San Diego, California, graduated on October 19, 1969. I, Sergeant Craig A. Tschetter, was awarded a USMC paperweight for placing third in a class of forty-five. Second place went to Sergeant Lanny A. Stevens, who received a USMC plaque. A gunnery sergeant (name unknown) received the first place honor, which was an official non-commissioned officer sword.

A paperweight doesn't sound like much of a reward after ten grueling weeks of the most difficult training I'd ever experienced, but I was ecstatic. Drill Instructor School was considered the premier leadership school in the Marine Corps, incorporating over five hundred hours of academics, physical training, and practical application over a ten-week period. We were taught military skills, conduct regulations, and procedures governing recruit training. In addition, the comprehensive leadership program included time management, communication skills, and counseling. However, the most difficult part was memorizing all the drill commands, maintaining an impeccable appearance, passing nearly impossible inspections, and completing an extremely demanding physical requirement.

Marines that earn the privilege of wearing the campaign cover "Smokey" carry with them one of the most challenging responsibilities of the Marine Corps. He must take young, naïve civilians straight off the streets of America and turn them into United States Marines.

During the sixties and seventies, we were given eight weeks to accomplish the task because of Vietnam's demand for troops. At times, one recruit training platoon overlapped with a second, which forced drill instructors to work without a break for days. Today recruit training is thirteen weeks, after which the drill instructors have one to five weeks off before picking up the next platoon.

On October 10, 1969, *Life* magazine featured an article entitled "The Pendleton Brig Rat: Ex-prisoners and Other Witnesses Report on the Brutalities Characterizing Life in a Marine Corps Prison," by Jack Fincher.

Within days, the same *Life* magazine team arrived at MCRD San Diego to prepare a story on recruit training. The timing of my graduation and their coverage was aligned perfectly. The class was selected for a series of photos depicting newly graduated drill instructors charged with training young men to become marines. The magazine's motive was clearly to uncover any form of cruelty or mistreatment of young recruits to further validate their claim of Marine Corps brutality. Needless to say, the entire depot was placed on alert and any form of mistreatment, including verbal harassment, was ordered to stop. Drill instructors were forced to change their tactics and by the time I was assigned my first platoon, they already adapted a means of stealth training. Discipline (thumping) was administered in the duty hut or in places where it would go unnoticed. A complete change from when Private Worley would be punched and slapped around in front of God and everyone. However, recruit training soon after returned to what it was like when Platoon 396 suffered the wrath of Gunnery Sgt. Kealoha, SSgt. Reeves, and Sgt. Furtato. It would be more appropriate to call the wrath a *modified state of shock.*

Recruit training in its simplest form was divided into three phases. During phase one the recruit could not possibly do anything right, even if he did it perfectly. By design, the first phase instilled the Marine Corps way of doing everything: the right way, the wrong way, and the Marine Corps way.

For example, going to the bathroom was referred to as a head call, a bed was a rack, a wall was a bulkhead, a gun was a weapon, and anyone other than another recruit was called "sir." During this phase the recruit was stripped of his civilian identity and forced to understand he now belonged to the Marine Corps. For some, that was an easy process, and others chose to be recalcitrant. This phase was also a time for drill instructors to evaluate who was a player and who was going to require additional motivation. It reflected the old saying: We'll either make you or break you.

Those who were required to be broken would be sent to one-day motivation platoon. Throughout this one day, the recruit was continually harassed, humiliated, and pushed to his physical limit in ways he never dreamed possible. If at the end of the day he was not persuaded by the Marine Corps ways, he was told he would stay as many days as it took to change him. If he remained for more than three days, he was sent to correctional custody platoon, where he would stay for one week.

In the correctional custody platoon, a recruit never marched anywhere—he only trotted (double time). He would carry two eight-pound hammers, one in each hand, hold them shoulder high, and learn what it's like to break rocks for eight hours each day. If after one week he was still not willing to become a marine, he would be discharged. If he was willing to become a marine, then he would join another platoon to pick up his training at the same point when he left his original platoon. It was extremely difficult for a recruit to join a new platoon because he was considered a failure. Many times the new platoon members treated him with rejection and often times beat him in his bed, under the cover of darkness after lights out. It was not uncommon for them to go AWOL or attempt suicide.

In this same period of training, the drill instructors were also relentlessly instilling unity as a platoon. If one recruit made a mistake, they all paid the price—whatever that may be. (It was during this phase I learned to hate Private Worley and resented my drill instructors the most.)

Phase one was extremely difficult for recruits, but it was designed that way in order to convert them from eighteen years of a civilian way of life to the Marine Corps way.

The team of drill instructors usually consisted of a gunnery sergeant or staff sergeant as the platoon commander and two additional sergeants. The platoon commander generally played the role of the father figure, while the other two played as the heavy or the light. The heavy was by far the most feared because recruits never ever got a break from harassment or punishment. For a recruit, the days the heavy was off duty were their best days; and the day he returned was, by far, their worst. I trained seven platoons in nineteen months, and with every platoon I was the heavy. My platoon commanders assigned me the position because I understood how to control power. They understood I was committed to making recruits recognize they were headed to a hostile environment, an environment not all of them would be coming home from. I only served with one platoon commander who had actually served in combat. They had all been to Vietnam, but they were in supply, motor transportation, or administration. One had a Meritorious Bronze Star, but not with a "V" for valor attached to it. I always felt they believed my commitment to recruits was different from theirs because of my time in combat.

During the time I was training my fourth platoon, I was told to report to the company office for a phone call. When I answered the phone, I was informed I would be decorated during the following week's parade and review ceremony.

I asked him, "What is the decoration for?"

He replied, "The medal is for your actions on June 15, 1968."

"What is the medal?"

"Well, according to the trail of paper, it started out as a Bronze Star with "V," but it was reduced to a Navy Commendation Medal with a Combat "V.""

The day of the ceremony, I was the only one being decorated. When the color guard and commanding officer in charge came to escort me to the front, my platoon couldn't believe it. In a matter of minutes, I went from being the biggest, meanest asshole to what they thought was some kind of war hero. I always felt they looked at me differently after hearing the citation read and watching the pinning of the medal.

Phase two was when recruits were trained to fire their weapon. Recruits along with the drill instructors were bused to Camp Pendleton's Eidson range for this phase of training. The first week was called "Snapping In," when recruits were taught various firing positions: sitting, prone, kneeling, etc. During the second week, they actually fired the weapon and qualified as a marksman. The three levels of qualifying were determined by the total score fired from various locations and positions. When a recruit scored two hundred twenty-five and above out of two hundred fifty possible target hits, he was classified as an expert marksman. A sharpshooter scored between two hundred and two hundred and twenty-four points, while a marksman scored between one hundred eighty and one ninety nine. The marksman badge awarded denoted the level of qualification. If a recruit didn't receive a shooting badge, he didn't qualify. To be non-qualified in the Marine Corps was like having leprosy. Recruits would cry because of the harassment, and some actually attempted suicide. It was a very stressful time for recruits and drill instructors. It was the only time during recruit training when a recruit was exposed to live ammunition. Some drill instructors were shot at while recruits were on the actual firing line. The movie *Full*

Metal Jacket is a very good example of a recruit shooting his drill instructor because of his constant abuse.

Phase three was also known as final phase and was devoted to finishing the recruit's skills academically, physically, and mentally. For the drill instructor, this phase was by far the easiest because if the instructors had done their job as a team, the platoon was something they were very proud of. The recruits knew graduation was around the corner, and they hoped to have family, a girlfriend, or friends present to share their accomplishment.

During my time on the drill field, there were two occasions during phase three when we picked up another platoon to begin training. This overlapping of platoons put overwhelming stress on the drill team.

For the drill instructors that were married, it was even more difficult. It was during this time that one of my platoon commanders was relieved and court-martialed for acts he committed. I felt sorry for him, but stress is not an excuse for the abuse of power over the lives of young recruits. I was given the black belt as the acting platoon commander during his absence.

During my final six weeks on the drill field, I was assigned as the platoon commander of casual platoon. This platoon was comprised of recruits being processed out of the Marine Corps for various reasons. They were a band of misfits who were undisciplined and could care less about anything that I said or did. Basically, I was a figurehead and marched them to and from the mess hall.

In 1971 the Marine Corps was throwing out 22 percent of what recruiters sent to either San Diego or Parris Island boot camps. Most were being discharged for past criminal records, drug abuse, homosexuality, or some type of health-related issue, such as a heart murmur. I remember one recruit was totally blind in one eye, but the recruiter told him not to say anything.

People who never experience boot camp, let alone Marine Corps boot camp, often considered it stupid, appalling, or even cruel. What these people fail to understand is what I know for a fact to be true: undisciplined warriors will either get killed or get other people killed. All the training in the world is not going to stop every warrior from being killed, but if they're not initiated to discipline during boot camp, they will not have a fighting chance.

In June of 1971, I was discharged a healthy, physically fit, disciplined, educated-by- combat, twenty-two-year-old young man. I had dreams of getting married, furthering my education, and living a life of joy and prosperity. At no time did I consider the possibility of my combat experiences altering my life. I was neither told nor warned—not once.

I have always claimed my time on the drill field was my savior from the effects of PTSD. I felt a part of the Marine Corps and not one of the unfortunate released into society with the hope of surviving. Little did I know nine years later that would all change and life would never be the same.

Navy Commendation Medal with Combat "V"

Sergeant Craig A. Tschetter

United States Marine Corps

CITATION: "For meritorious service while serving in various capacities with Company I, Third Battalion, Fifth Marines, First Marine Division in connection with combat operations against the enemy in the Republic of Vietnam from 23 November 1967 to 27 July 1969. Throughout this period, Sergeant Tschetter performed his duties in an exemplary and highly professional manner. Participating in several major combat operations as well as in numerous small-unit activities, he repeatedly distinguished himself by his courage and composure under fire. Initially assigned as a Rifleman and subsequently reassigned as the Company Radio Operator, he expeditiously accomplished all appointed tasks and consistently provided his unit with outstanding support. On 15 June 1968, Company I was heavily engaged in combat with a large North Vietnamese Army force in Quang Nam Province. Alertly observing several casualties who were in need of immediate medical attention, Sergeant Tschetter informed the battalion commander of the situation and requested medical evacuation helicopters. Fearlessly maneuvering throughout the fire-swept terrain to more accurately ascertain the hostile position, he was instrumental in ensuring the timely delivery of devastatingly accurate artillery fire upon the enemy and thereby contributed significantly to the successful evacuation of the casualties and defeat of the North Vietnamese Army force. As a result of his diligent and resourceful efforts, the operational effectiveness of his unit was greatly enhanced. By his initiative, superb professionalism and loyal devotion to duty, Sergeant Tschetter earned the respect of all who served with him and upheld the finest traditions of the Marine Corps and of the United States Naval Service. The Combat "V" Distinguishing Device is authorized."

CHAPTER NINETEEN

"Men who went to do the incomprehensibly difficult job their nation sent them to do and did it proudly, did it well, and all too often did it thanklessly." —*Lt. Col. Dave Grossman*

During the summer of 1973, as a student at South Dakota State University, I decided to enroll in two classes. I was looking to accelerate my time spent getting my pre-mortuary requirement completed. Both classes were difficult for me, but I needed them as part of my requirements. The one course was taught by a professor from Wisconsin who returned every year to teach a particular class. She was a wonderful, compassionate professor and perfect for a veteran without much prior knowledge in the subject. I never missed a class the entire summer and worked hard to make certain I obtained a good grade because it was important to my future studies in mortuary science. What happened to cause my grade to be an "incomplete" is still confusing to me, but, regardless, that was my final grade. She had written a note in my file for the department head stating that she didn't understand why I chose not to attend the second day of the final exam. I had no clue it was a two-day exam, and if I had, I would have certainly been there. Why I didn't know remains a mystery to me.

With limited options and mostly out of confusion, I went to see the department head because my professor had already returned to Wisconsin. He was alone in the laboratory when I approached him hoping to find the answer to my grade. I respectfully introduced myself and asked if he could help me understand my incomplete.

He retrieved my file, opened it, and curtly said, "You didn't finish the final exam."

"What do you mean?" I asked.

"The final was a two-day exam."

"I didn't know that. What can I do?"

"You goddamn Vietnam vets; all you look for is handouts," he snapped.

Those were the words I heard in response to a simple question regarding a grade in 1973. It hurt me more than he could have ever imagined.

I, who was more mature than the other students because of war, would have no reason to want a handout. I had been humbled by combat, was married with a child, and working to obtain an education. Why would I want a handout? If anyone did, it would be all the young snots sitting in classes with me wasting their parents' money. They lacked discipline, self-confidence, and maturity. Not me. Yet, he chose to blister me with what I considered prejudice and disrespectful language. It was only the beginning of what would eventually become an extremely difficult life of learning to cope with the residual effects of having served in Vietnam.

Campus life during the seventies was filled with protest, outrage, and hatred on every level toward the war. It was especially difficult for me when individuals spoke about Vietnam in ways that degraded the war effort. At times, I overheard conversations or witnessed protests that would cause my anger to surge. Other times, classroom discussions would make me furious, but I knew better than to speak up. I just listened. I understood the nation was against the war, but I wasn't ready to admit all the pain and suffering I had experienced and witnessed was for nothing. I still believed, as a nation, we needed to do our part in containing communism.

Right or wrong, I still believed in the core values that made our country great, and I wanted more than anything to be right. Plus, it had been just over a year since I was training recruits to face the hostile environment I had faced, and I believed deeply in the Marine Corps training.

So for me, during my time in college, I was steadfast in how I felt about Vietnam even though I chose not to take a stand in favor of the war. I preferred to avoid confrontation and go about my business of gaining an education.

Life still wasn't easy for me. There were the constant reminders of Vietnam on television, reminding me of things I really didn't want to think about anymore. However, life seemed pleasant with Della, a loving wife, and newborn daughter to give me the love I needed to help block the thoughts of war. Our love ran deep, and together we felt there wasn't anything we couldn't accomplish or withstand together. Those feelings stayed with us for years, even though prior to our marriage I had experienced two minor breakdowns. At the time I considered them more frustrating than concerning. What I failed to realize was how much of a warning sign they really were.

In both cases Della was present and both involved an individual who was a braggart, exaggerating the truth about Vietnam. During one occasion I held in my hand a glass ketchup bottle (upside down by the neck) ready to back-hand it across the braggart's face. I actually planned what I wanted to do, how I would do it, and the choice of weapon. My military training made the planning easy. The rage in me was so strong I was ready to throw my life away by killing him. Instead, I set the bottle down, left the establishment, went outside, and wept beside my car. I was emotionally dis-traught and shockingly aware that I still possessed the tools to kill. Della soon found me, threw her arms around me, and asked, "What's wrong?" I didn't want to tell her; she might have seen me as weak or unstable. I was embarrassed for being in tears. It wasn't exactly how I planned my future wife to see me. All I could say was I needed to leave before I did something I would regret. I'm not certain she under-stood what I meant, but she didn't ask any more questions. I realized something wasn't right but still had no clue to what that might mean.

When the first troops started pulling out of Vietnam in 1973, I felt like we must have failed to stop communism even though I realized we negotiated an end. I was overjoyed to watch the return of our POWs and actually teared up on more than one occasion.

Then came the disastrous fall of Saigon in 1975, which was followed by the occupation of South Vietnam by communist North Vietnam, and I began to realize it was all for naught. Our country's leaders started openly admitting the flawed nature of a policy of containment. All the dead, wounded, missing, and scarred-for-life warriors appeared to have no meaning. It was as if the entire war were a movie with a beginning and an end—an end I found full of unanswered questions, misunderstandings, and a disturbing distrust for what I thought was a noble cause. It seemed unfair or as if I had been tricked somehow.

Then in 1977 I knew for certain the country played over 2.7 million soldiers for fools when President Carter granted full amnesty to over one hundred thousand civilians who dodged the draft. They either fled the country or went into hiding only to be completely forgiven and granted full rights as United States citizens. It made me furious. "How could this happen?" I kept asking Della. It was totally unfair to all Americans who served with dignity and pride for our country. It was the turning point for my anger against our government and for what I thought we stood for. I was mad at the president, Congress, and most of all, the people of this nation who allowed it to happen. What did I do about it? Nothing. Instead, I let it fester in my mind until one day in 1980 everything changed.

All across America the Iranian hostage crisis was front-page news. Americans showed their deep concern and love of their country's fellow man by tying large yellow ribbons around trees. It was impressive for all to see. Ironically, it was those same yellow ribbons that caused me to fall into a deep, dark pit of depression. All I could see for my life was a circle of light the size of the opening of the pit. Odd as it may seem, that's exactly how I felt.

West Blvd, Rapid City, SD (early 1980's)

The ribbons triggered my old feelings of anger and hatred toward the people of this country for their unfairness. I couldn't understand how they could pour out such a meaningful expression of concern for a few hostages while completely rebuking the Vietnam veteran. I felt they were betraying not only me but also all the buddies I lost and all the pain and suffering we went through; it was completely unjust.

Everything from Vietnam started piling up in my mind: faces, places, murdered civilians, young soldiers I killed, fire fights, exploding mortars, snipers, sappers…It would not stop cluttering up in my mind, regardless of what I tried. Eventually, it turned into an out-of-control, terrifying obsession cast with my ghosts of war.

My life as a husband, a father, and a professional dis-appeared. What was once an enjoyable person suddenly became this withdrawn, quick-to-anger recluse. I resigned myself to the solitude of our bedroom and oftentimes would sit in the corner holding my head crying tears of frustration.

Not only would the war not leave my mind, but it also scared me. I couldn't stop thinking about what I might do to myself.

Finally, I came to a point where I could see little if any reason to live. My entire world was crashing in on me for reasons I couldn't understand or control. My recurring thought was to end my life in order to rid myself of the torment. I thought of ways to die by recalling the various forms of suicide I dealt with as a funeral director—how women took the less aggressive route with pills or carbon monoxide while men usually used a gun or hanged themselves. I was close—very close—to ending it all. I was beginning to feel like I was already walking with the dead....

Dr. Ching met me at the door to his office and introduced himself. The conversation quickly centered on his biggest concern: life-threatening thoughts. Tears began to fall from embarrassment and fear of what was happening in my life. When I told him about my time in Vietnam, he acted like he'd heard it all before. But, when I mentioned the yellow ribbons, he moved closer, placed his arms on the desk, and asked, "What do you mean by yellow ribbons?" he asked.

After hearing my explanation, he assured me he could help me, but first I needed to understand something. He said, "Your memories are never ever going to leave you. You will have them for the rest of your life. The sooner you accept what I've said, the sooner your life will begin to change. The Veterans Administration Hospital can provide counseling, group therapy, or medications, and for some veterans, we've found that writing about their experiences helps them to cope."

I suddenly began to feel I had a chance to survive when before I could see no positive solution to my torment. Instead of ending my life, I realized there was truly a way to go on living. I didn't need to lose my family and all the things I had worked to obtain. I felt fortunate to have made the decision to seek help. It was the most wonderful and amazing decision I ever made. It's why I'm here—writing these words.

Today, I see a Veterans Administration Hospital psychiatrist every three months to maintain an adequate supply of medicine to control panic attacks, depression, and PTSD. The medicine is my leveler, providing me with the calm I need to live a full life. Individuals who know me personally see me as an outgoing, fun guy. What they don't know is when they talk to me or when we're playing golf, I'm having thoughts about Vietnam. The thoughts don't bother me anymore because of the medications; they're just there. It may seem difficult to believe, but it's true.

People often ask me when I was in Vietnam. I usually tell them from November 23, 1967, until July 27, 1969. What I really want to tell them is the truth. I want to say, "Fifteen minutes ago."

I can't speak for issues facing veterans of recent wars, but I do know our country has undergone dramatic change in the way they treat veterans since the sixties. Honestly, I'm not only happy for the veteran, but also proud of our country. The country now realizes combat will produce damaging consequences to a warrior—both psychologically and spiritually.

Do I wish it would have happened during my era? Absolutely. But just experiencing a small taste of respect for being a veteran of Vietnam can be very humbling.

A few years ago I was sitting in the waiting area prior to boarding a flight when a soldier dressed in camouflaged desert utilities sat down a few seats away. It was obvious he was either going or coming back from a deployment.

I didn't speak to him. I just observed his actions more out of curiosity than anything else. I couldn't even see what rank he was and at the time, didn't care. A few minutes later a young lady in her early twenties took a seat between us leaving two seats to her left from him and two seats between us. At no time was there any conversation between the three of us until a line formed in front of us with passengers boarding another flight.

A young lady in line spotted the uniformed soldier and approached him in tears and said, "Excuse me, sir, but can I hug you? My husband is in Iraq and your uniform...well, I really need a hug." The soldier appeared very surprised, stood, and the two hugged as she wept. She eventually stepped back and thanked him saying, "I needed that more than you will ever realize. Thank you." Then she departed.

When he sat down, I leaned forward looking around the young lady between us and said, "That was amazing. Does that happen often?"

He kindly replied, "I've read about those things, heard others talk about them, but I've never before experienced it."

I said, "I'm happy for you.

Before he could respond the young lady between us asked, "Why?"

I explained our country was different back then, and veterans were not treated with respect, but instead were scorned for having gone to fight in Vietnam. It was clear because of her age she was confused and obviously unfamiliar with the events of the sixties as well as Vietnam.

The soldier leaned forward and said, "I wish it would have been different back then because the Vietnam veterans deserved their country's respect. What branch did you serve with in Vietnam?"

"The Marine Corps," I replied.

For the next thirty minutes, no one said another word until the soldier stood to board his plane. It was at that time I noticed he was a lieutenant colonel in the medical corps of the Army.

He said, "Well, I need to leave. This is my second deployment to Iraq as a surgeon." He then snapped to attention, looked me in the eye and said, "Marine, thank you for your service during the Vietnam War." He then saluted me, gathered his gear, and walked away. I was humbled beyond words.

The young girl looked at my watering eyes and said, "Wow, that's one of the coolest things I've ever seen."

To be totally healed of my experiences, I fully recognize, will not be possible. However, small encounters like I just described can mean so much in learning to cope on a daily basis. But when something major happens beyond explanation the healing can be huge—like an unexpected phone call I received in 2000.

Della handed me the phone while covering the receiver and said, "I think it's a telemarketer because he has a Southern accent." The voice on the other end asked, "Is this Craig Tschetter?"

"Yes," I replied.

"Well, we served together in Vietnam. My name is Curtis Eidson."

"I don't remember or even know a Curtis Eidson."

"Well, you were Captain Kolakowski's radio operator when he was killed on June 15, 1968, correct?"

Suddenly, a chill went through me, and I said, "Yes."

"Well, brother you have been found. Welcome home. Are you on the line?"

"Yes."

"Go to www.usmcvietvet.org and under photos you will see the picture of you I've been circulating around the world for the past three years. Contact me tomorrow."

"I will. I promise."

He had been trying to find me to invite me to a Third Battalion, Fifth Marines reunion. That one phone call has, without a doubt, given me the most healing of any one thing in my entire life. Because of that call, I've met many of the men I served with, cried with, fought with, and was certain I would never see again in my lifetime. When you look into the eyes of a man you've thought about for thirty some years, all you can do is hug him and cry. I did it over and over, as they did with me.

For the first time since leaving Vietnam, I was able to have a conversation with someone who actually understood and cared. It was gratifying and at the same time surreal.

My life in Vietnam suddenly meant something again; it was no longer just a haunting experience. The reunion brought a revelation that I wasn't alone in my thoughts and fears. We shared story after story over and over until someone told another. We talked about people we had forgotten and names surfaced we had long forgotten about. There were times it seemed like a dream, but reality set in and I actually was with buddies I had no clue were even alive. I was elated. Every year except one, Della went with me; and during the second reunion, our children joined us, making it even the more special. I look forward to each year with anticipation of meeting a new face that was recently found—just like I was in 2001.

* * *

The process of chasing my ghosts has been, at times, very difficult, but it's also been a learning experience I feel I need to share with others. It's a large part of why I've chosen to write this book—so others understand that once a soldier commits to serve their country and fight in combat, it doesn't just end. Life doesn't work that way. The price one pays is in direct proportion to how war treated him and how well prepared he was before. For some it's peace; for others, it's a nightmare. For me, who at age eighteen made the decision to serve his country, it has been an amazing journey—a journey filled with innocence, anguish, and coping. I'm not ashamed of my decision to serve. I'm neither sorry for my actions nor do I feel any guilt. I'm simply grateful to be alive.

AFTERWORD

L t. Col. Dave Grossman's book *On Killing* speaks volumes about not only the act of killing during war but who does the killing and the latent effects. He writes about a World War II study that notes 2 percent of combat soldiers are predisposed to be "aggressive psychopaths" and apparently do not experience the normal resistance to killing and the resultant psychiatric casualties associated with combat. Lt. Col. Grossman believes a more accurate conclusion would be that there is 2 percent of the male population that if pushed or if given a legitimate reason will kill without regret or remorse. That being said, let me quote one of my marine buddies I served with in Vietnam: "Jesus, Tschetter, think about it, where could we have gone at age nineteen and have the right to legally kill people?" That was his legitimate reason. It's what he was willing to die for—the excitement of chasing and killing the ultimate animal (another human being).

One of the struggles a writer must deal with when writing a non-fiction book is how to deal with truthfulness. For me, it was never a matter of whether I should tell the truth; it was all about how to tell the truth without implications. Compromising someone's identity or actions was at stake. However, even then, there are special circumstances that entitle some writers, including me, to disclose the facts.

The fact I needed to disclose was the senseless murder of a Vietnamese civilian mother and her two small children. Those twenty seconds traumatized my life forever. There's not a day I don't think about it or visualize it. What my squad leader wantonly did that afternoon was criminal—I know it, he knows it, and one other marine knows it.

A few years ago I shared the story with another marine who, as an officer, commanded an infantry company in Vietnam. He was not part of my battalion but clearly understood what I was talking about. He asked, "Well, why in the hell didn't you report it?"

I tried to help him understand my fear of being killed by my squad leader, to which he replied, "He'd been gone to the brig before he could have done that." I thought, *Well that's pretty easy for you say, having not been in my boots*. Instead of trying to empathize with me, he arrogantly reminded me I had broken rules set forth by the Geneva Convention. He chose to make me feel less of a marine and more of a coward. Needless to say, I was not pleased with his comments.

I've tried various ways to locate my former squad leader and everything leads to a dead end. I can find no record of how to spell his name, and no one in the company can remember either. It was just a few years ago I learned his first name. One of India Company's lieutenants told me his name and that before leaving Vietnam he begged the officer to sign papers allowing him to return. The lieutenant refused his request on the principle that if you were lucky enough to survive one tour your chances of surviving a second would be slim—a tenet he lived by with all who requested extended tours.

What my squad leader did that day will be with me forever. He gave me no say. I've learned to live with the memory of their faces, their actions filled with fear, the pooling of blood on the red dirt, and the words, "Let's go."

To kill the enemy during war is justified by the Rules of Engagement, but what I was forced to witness was nothing more than a legitimate reason to kill during a war that was misguided from the start. May God rest our souls.

* * *

I also want to make a few comments about the reunion I mentioned throughout the book. It was actually an idea that stemmed from a small band of India Company members who met for a weekend in Waco, Georgia, several years ago. Curtis Eidson took it upon himself along with his wife, Brenda, to attempt to locate other members of India Company for various reasons. It soon evolved into the entire company personnel of Third Battalion, Fifth Marines.

The first reunion was held in 2000 with a small group gathering for a few days at a state park outside of La Grange, Georgia. Della and I began attending in 2001. Over the years it has grown to well over one hundred and fifty marines along with their wives, children, and special friends. The location has changed over time because the group needed more space; South Carolina and Kentucky served as sites. It continues to grow, but the attrition rate is having an effect on the numbers.

The most important event of the reunion occurs on the Saturday of the reunion when the battalion honors one of our brothers lost during the war. His family is invited to attend the ceremony and is presented with a shadow box containing the American flag and all the medals awarded to the fallen marine. In many cases, the family had never received the medals and is overjoyed to see the decorations earned by their loved one for the first time. It's a very moving experience for all. The only expense the family incurs is transportation to the reunion site; the battalion covers all of their expenses once they arrive.

On Labor Day weekend in 2009, I flew to Oregon and met with Tim and Karen Salisbury, the brother of my friend Jim who was killed on June 18, 1968. I wanted to keep the promise I made years before to visit Jim's family, plus I wanted to invite Tim and Karen to South Carolina to honor Jim. I had recommended Jim to the company as someone I felt we should honor; they agreed.

Tim and Karen accepted the invitation, and in June of 2010, India Company honored Jim. I spoke on behalf of the company honoring Jim's bravery and his sacrifice to this great country. It was extremely moving for me, as he was truly a great friend. For the family, they couldn't believe there were people who even thought of Jim after all these years, and they felt blessed to meet them.

Today, we remain very close friends. Karen calls me her favorite marine, and Tim is like a brother. I feel blessed when we share time together, which since 2009, has been every year I visit our son in Oregon.

Glossary

AK47	North Vietnamese and Viet Cong rifle
AO	Area of Operation | Aeriel Observer
ARVN	Army of the Republic of Vietnam
B40	Rocket-propelled grenade launcher used by NVA/VC
Bird	Aircraft, most often a helicopter | The author's nickname in Vietnam
Bush	Field area where combat troops operated
C4	Plastic explosive, usually in one-pound bars
CH46	Type of a Sikorsky helicopter with twin rotors.
Chopper	Helicopter
CP	Command Post
C-rations	Cardboard box meals
DMZ	Demilitarized zone: 17th parallel dividing Vietnam
Get Some	Fifth Marine's jargon "to kill the enemy"
Gook	Korean slang for "person"
Purple Heart	Medal awarded for being wounded
Hooch	Vietnamese villager's place of living or home
KIA	Killed in action
LZ	Landing zone
M16	Standard issue weapon for U.S. military personnel

Medevac	Medical evacuation of a wounded or ill person. *Emergency* "near death," *priority* "seriously wounded," and *routine* either "ambulatory or dead"
MCRD	Marine Corps Recruit Depot
NVA	North Vietnamese Army or soldier
OPCON	Operational Control
R&R	Rest and Relaxation leave
Sapper	North Vietnamese Army Special Forces
Song	Vietnamese word for "river"
Spooky	C130 aircraft used to drop luminary flares
Strobe	Small handheld light
TAOR	Tactical Area of Responsibility
VC	Viet Cong (South Vietnamese communist)
WESTPAC	Western Pacific
Zone of the Unknown	Author's phrase to describe a semi-conscious state of confusion

SOUTH VIETNAM

ADMINISTRATIVE DIVISIONS
AND MILITARY REGIONS

JUNE 1967

- - - - - International boundary
· · · · · · · Province boundary
∞∞∞∞∞ Military corps boundary
⊛ National capital
⊛ Province capital
DA LAT Autonomous municipality

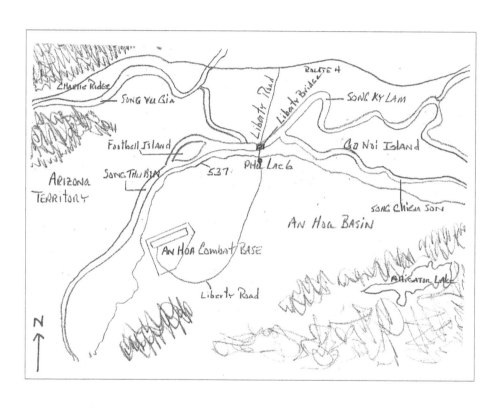